SCIENCE
FOUNDATIONS

Radioactivity

SCIENCE FOUNDATIONS

SCIENCE
FOUNDATIONS

Radioactivity

P. ANDREW KARAM, Ph.D., AND BEN P. STEIN

CHELSEA HOUSE
PUBLISHERS
An imprint of Infobase Publishing

Radioactivity

JUN **1 8** 2009

Chelsea House
An imprint of Infobase Publishing
132 West 31st Street
New York NY 10001

Library of Congress Cataloging-in-Publication Data
Karam, P. Andrew.
 Radioactivity / P. Andrew Karam and Ben P. Stein.
   p. cm. — (Science foundations)
 Includes bibliographical references and index.
 ISBN 978-1-60413-016-4 (hardcover)
 1. Radioactivity—Popular works. 2. Radiation—Popular works. I. Stein, Ben P. II. Title.
 QC795.26.K37 2009
 539.2—dc22   2008038067

Chelsea House books are available at special discounts when purchased in bulk quantities for businesses, associations, institutions, or sales promotions. Please call our Special Sales Department in New York at (212) 967-8800 or (800) 322-8755.

You can find Chelsea House on the World Wide Web at
http://www.chelseahouse.com

Text design by Kerry Casey
Cover design by Ben Peterson

Printed in the United States of America

Bang EJB 10 9 8 7 6 5 4 3 2 1

This book is printed on acid-free paper.

All links and Web addresses were checked and verified to be correct at the time of publication. Because of the dynamic nature of the Web, some addresses and links may have changed since publication and may no longer be valid.

Contents

Radiation Basics

Everyone is **radioactive**. For that matter, so is almost everything in the human world—bananas in the kitchen, the bricks and concrete in homes, smoke detectors, and most things that can be eaten, worn, played with, or touched every day. And, as if that is not enough, the outside world contains even more radiation, from the rocks and soil, from the atmosphere, and even from outer space. No one can escape radiation—anywhere in the whole universe. Radiation has been in the universe since it began, and it has been on Earth since it first formed. Everything that has ever lived on Earth has been exposed to radiation, and virtually everything on Earth is at least a little bit radioactive.

An object is radioactive if it naturally releases high-energy particles such as **X-rays**. These high-energy particles are called **radiation**. Everything (this book included) is likely to have something in it that gives off high-energy radiation, even if it is in tiny amounts.

OK, so everything is radioactive. But this does not mean much without explaining what *radioactive* means. And that means learning a little bit of the science behind radioactivity, and learning a little bit of the terminology that helps to understand the science.

ATOMS

Several thousand years ago, a Greek philosopher named Democritus was enjoying the smell of some bread when he started to think about how, if the bread was cut, he would have some smaller pieces. Then, if he cut those, he would have even smaller pieces. And, as he kept cutting, the pieces would get smaller and smaller and smaller. So, Democritus wondered, how many times could he cut the bread? It occurred to him that he could not just keep cutting the bread forever; at some point, the bits of bread would be so small that they simply could not be cut any more. He thought that it made sense to think that there was a size limit—that he could only make pieces of bread that were so small, but no smaller. When he got to the smallest piece—the piece that could not be cut any further—Democritus called it "uncuttable"; the Greek word for this is **atom**.

Human understanding of atoms has changed a lot in the last few thousand years. The actual world of atoms is far more interesting, and harder to understand, than the ancient Greeks could comprehend. There is not just one type of atom—there are now over 115 known varieties. Atoms can join together into larger units known as **molecules**. Bread, for example, is made of many kinds of atoms and molecules. Plus, atoms are, in reality, "cuttable." It is possible to split atoms into pieces, unleashing large amounts of energy that can be used for war or peace.

As scientists now know, atoms contain a core that is known as the **nucleus.** The nucleus contains particles called **protons** and **neutrons**. Protons and neutrons weigh about the same. But while neutrons have no electrical charge, protons have a positive electrical charge. Meanwhile, the nucleus is surrounded by a cloud of particles called **electrons**, which have a negative electrical charge. Even though an electron is almost 2,000 times lighter than a proton, the negative electrical charge of one electron is just as strong as the positive charge of one proton, so their charges balance out each other. In most atoms, the total number of protons is the same as the number of electrons, so the positive and negative charges cancel each other perfectly; such an atom is called "neutral."

Magnets can help illustrate what takes place in an atom. Sometimes a magnet will push another magnet away because the magnets are lined up so their two north poles, or two south poles, are next to each other. In other words, similar magnetic poles push each other away. It is the same with electrical charges. The positive charges in protons tend to push the protons away from each other, just as two north magnetic poles will push each other away. To have an atom with more than one proton in it, there must be something that can overcome this force. This is where the neutrons come in.

Neutrons act like glue to help hold an atomic nucleus together. Neutrons in a nucleus exert a force (called the **strong nuclear force**) that pulls together everything in the nucleus. Protons also have the strong nuclear force to pull everything together, but the strong nuclear force of the protons alone is not strong enough to counteract the electrical force that pushes protons apart. Neutrons make it possible to keep many protons in the same place. Thanks to neutrons, there are atoms with anywhere from 1 to over 100 protons in the nucleus.

The number of protons in a nucleus determines what type of atom, or **element**, it is. For example, a nucleus with one proton is the element hydrogen, and a nucleus with 92 protons is uranium, the heaviest element that naturally occurs in large quantities. (Trace quantities of plutonium, which is heavier than uranium, have been found in uranium ore deposits, but only a few atoms at a time.) Scientists in experimental laboratories have artificially created elements with more than 92 protons. For some of the most recently created elements, with 116 and 118 protons, scientists have not yet even agreed on their names.

When an atom has too much energy, it needs to get rid of the energy. The atom also needs just the right numbers of neutrons and protons so it will stay together: If there are too many or too few neutrons for the number of protons in the nucleus, the atom will usually either convert a proton to a neutron, or a neutron to a proton. An atom can often accomplish both of these tasks at the same time, and that process is called **radioactive decay**.

When an atom decays, it releases particles and often transforms into a lighter element. For example, uranium decays into thorium, which is a lighter element. There are several different types of radioactive decay. Each kind of decay releases a different type of particle.

RADIOACTIVITY AND RADIATION

Protons want to push each other apart. Neutrons want to hold protons together. So it is easy to see that an atom might simply fly apart if it does not have enough neutrons. Technically, an atom with too many protons (or too few neutrons) has too much energy from the electrical force of protons pushing against each other. But what if there are too many neutrons (or not enough protons)? In this case, there is too much of the strong nuclear force, and the atom still has too much energy.

The only way to have a stable atom is to have the right balance between the forces carried by protons and neutrons. Too many neutrons, or too few, and the atom has too much energy. This is what makes an atom unstable, and unstable atoms are radioactive.

If an atom has too many neutrons (or not enough protons) to be stable, what can it do? One possibility is for the atoms to change some neutrons into protons. But there is a problem: A neutron has zero total electrical charge, and a proton has positive charge, but the atom cannot change the total amount of electrical charge it has. So what happens is that the neutron decays into two particles: a positively charged proton—which stays in the atom—and a negatively charged electron, which flies out of the atom. The positive electrical charge from the proton and negative charge from the electron balance out each other. And the electron that flies out of the atom solves another problem: It also helps the atom to shed some of its extra energy. By simply expelling an electron, the atom can solve two problems at once. This type of radiation—the release of an electron—is called **beta radiation**, and it is one of the principal kinds of radiation.

Some atoms start off with too much energy of their own. These kinds of atoms are unstable, or radioactive. Unstable atoms get rid of this extra energy by giving off radiation. And radioactive materials are simply collections of unstable atoms.

There are other forms of radiation in addition to the beta radiation mentioned above. Heavy atomic elements like radium, uranium, and plutonium do more than just turn a single proton into a single neutron, or vice versa. They are more likely to give off clusters of protons and neutrons—precisely two protons and two neutrons, called **alpha particles**. Alpha radiation is a second kind of

Table 1.1 Properties of Radiation					
Type of radiation	What is it?	How heavy is it?	How much electrical charge?	Distance it will travel in the body	How harmful is it?
Alpha	An object consisting of two neutrons and two protons	Massive— about 8,000 times the mass of an electron, or 4 times the mass of a neutron or proton	+2 (twice that of a proton)	About 1 cell	Very harmful on the inside of the body, completely harmless outside the body
Beta	An electron	Very light— about 1/2000 the mass of a single neutron or proton	+1 or −1 (the same strength as an electron)	About 1 centimeter	Harmful in large amounts, not very harmful in small amounts
Gamma	A high-energy form of light	No mass	No charge	Through the whole body	

radiation. **Gamma radiation** is a third kind. Also known as **gamma rays**, this form of radiation is just like light rays or X-rays, but with much more energy.

Where Radiation Comes From

Radiation is everywhere on Earth and in the universe. Where does it all come from? Radiation comes from radioactive atoms, but there is much more to it than that. A more interesting question is to ask where the radioactive atoms on Earth come from.

Radioactive atoms (and many of the atoms that make up the human body) come from exploded stars. All stars are originally composed of only the two lightest elements (hydrogen and helium), but over time, they form heavier elements, as heavy as iron. Eventually, stars run out of the hydrogen and helium fuel that allows them to shine. When they run out of fuel, larger stars can collapse in on themselves. As a star collapses, it creates a spectacular explosion called a supernova. In the few moments that a star squishes itself into a hot, dense ball, the star forms even heavier elements—all the way up to uranium and beyond. When a star collapses, its outer layers bounce off of its core and explode, spraying its heavier elements into the surrounding space.

Scientists think that about 6 billion years ago, a large star exploded near the Sun. Over the next billion years, some of the elements from this nearby exploding star would have collected together in a great interstellar cloud that eventually would have collapsed to form the solar system, around 4.5 billion years ago. This interstellar cloud would have included every bit of what eventually became the Earth, plus some of the radioactive atoms that had formed in the now-dead star.

Much of that radioactivity, from whatever star it came from, is still on Earth, and most of the Earth's natural radioactivity now exists in rocks and soils. This natural radioactivity in the rocks begins with the atomic elements uranium, thorium, and potassium. But radioactive atoms do not last forever. They tend to decay, or break down, into lighter elements. These **decay products** can be either radioactive or nonradioactive. A radioactive decay product breaks down again into even lighter elements. A nonradioactive product is **stable**, meaning that it no longer decays into anything else.

Radioactive potassium decays directly to either calcium or argon, both of which are nonradioactive (stable). But the decay of uranium and thorium is much more interesting: These elements decay through a series of radioactive elements (including **radon** and **radium**) until reaching stable lead. Natural uranium, thorium, and their radioactive byproducts, in addition to the radioactive potassium, account for a good deal of the radiation on Earth. And some of the radon that comes from the decay of uranium and thorium provides even more natural radiation. Together, these provide about three-quarters of the radiation that humans receive from nature.

Still more radiation comes from radioactive potassium that is inside the human body. Even more comes from outer space in the form of **cosmic radiation** from the sun and elsewhere in the galaxy.

These account for about one-seventh and one-tenth of natural radiation **dose**, respectively. In units of radiation dose (called **Sieverts** in the international system, or **rem** in standard measurement—1 Sievert is equal to 100 rem), each human being on Earth is exposed to nearly 0.003 Sieverts (0.3 rem) annually from natural sources.

Man-made sources also expose people to radiation. Medicine is the largest of these sources. X-rays, nuclear medicine procedures, CT scans, and so forth expose patients each year to, on average, about 3.3 mSv (milliSieverts, or thousandths of a Sievert) or 330 mrem (millirems, or thousandths of a rem), adding about 50% more radiation **exposure** in addition to what people naturally receive. This amount is increasing as people make more and more use of these often lifesaving procedures, though scientists are at the same time trying to reduce the amount of radiation from medical procedures. In addition, some consumer products (such as smoke detectors) also contain trace amounts of radioactivity, amounting to nearly .1 mSv (10 mrem) each year. By comparison, **nuclear reactors**, radioactive waste, fallout from nuclear weapons testing, and all other sources of man-made radiation expose the human population to another .02 mSv (2 mrem) each year on average.

When this is all added up, humans in North America are exposed to about 6.3 mSv (630 mrem) each year, nearly 3.0 of which comes from nature and the rest from man-made sources.

Using Radiation and Radioactivity

Radiation is not only everywhere on Earth, it can also be tremendously useful, and society uses it extensively. The major areas where it is used are in research, medicine, and industry.

In medicine, radiation is used in an amazing number of ways. It can help doctors look inside the body to diagnose broken bones, cancer, and other diseases. Not only can radiation help doctors "see," it can also cure a number of diseases. Radiation has been used in medicine for over a century now, and it is one of the most valuable tools that a doctor has. Chapter 3 provides much more information on how doctors use radiation to help their patients.

Scientists also use radiation extensively in their research, mostly in medical and biological research. In most cases, the scientists are interested in finding out, for example, if a new medicine travels to the right organ, or how nutrients are used by a cell. Radioactivity is likely to find new uses in medicine and research for many years to come.

Radiation and radioactivity are even used in industry. Radiation gets weaker and weaker while passing through an object to the

How to Detect Radiation: The Geiger Counter

Just a decade after discovering radioactivity, scientists invented a good device for measuring it, which is still in use today in modern versions: It is called a **Geiger counter**. In its simplest form, this device is a metal tube filled with a gas made up of atoms.

When high-energy radiation such as an X-ray or gamma ray strikes an atom, it can remove an electron from that atom—a process that is called **ionization**. An electron has a negative electrical charge, and the remaining atom, which is called an **ion**, now has a positive electrical charge. Normally, the negatively charged electron and the positively charged ion would be attracted to each other and so end up back together again, a process known as recombination. However, a Geiger counter prevents this recombination from happening.

Inside the Geiger counter's metal tube is a wire connected to a battery. If the wire is given a strong enough positive charge, the electron will rush toward it, and the ion will rush to the tube itself, which is negatively charged. When this happens, the electron and the ion bump into other atoms hard enough to ionize them too. Then the electrons and ions from the new ion pairs will bump into still more atoms, causing even more ionization. This happens again and again, until almost every atom in the Geiger tube is ionized. Then, when they reach the wire, the electrons travel through it until they reach the wall of the tube, where they combine with the positive ions to form electrically neutral atoms again. During this process, the electrons also pass through a monitoring device that registers each innermost part because the outer layers absorb a lot of it. For example, suppose a factory is making steel sheets that are supposed to be precisely 0.5 inches (1.19 centimeters) thick. This factory can put a radioactive substance above a sheet and a radiation detector beneath it. If the detector shows that the radiation is too high, it

one of them as a "count." So, if the Geiger counter is reading, say, 1,000 counts per minute, it means that this whole process is happening 1,000 times in every minute, or about 16 to 17 times each second. Some Geiger counters register each count as an audible "click"; others show the radioactivity levels in a visual display.

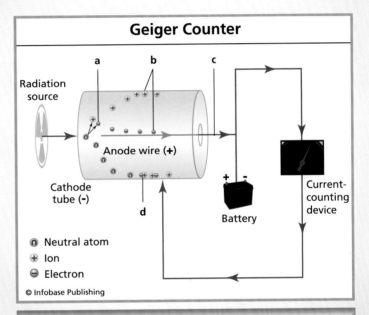

Figure 1.1 A Geiger counter measures radioactivity. Radiation causes a neutral atom to ionize, resulting in an ion and a free electron (a). The negatively charged electrons are attracted to a positively charged anode wire; positively charged ions are attracted to the negatively charged sides of the cathode tube (b). Electrons travel along the anode wire where a current counting device counts the number of electrons that pass (c). The anode wire returns the electrons to the cathode tube, where they recombine with ions to form neutral atoms once again (d).

Sources of Radiation

The universe is filled with radiation, and all living things on Earth are constantly exposed to it. Most of this radiation is natural, but some of the radiation exposure is from man-made sources.

Natural Radiation

All rocks and soils contain radioactivity in the form of trace amounts of uranium, thorium, and a type of radioactive atom called potassium-40 (K-40). Some areas have higher levels of radiation than others—in Hawaii, for example, the local rocks are much less radioactive than they are in Wyoming or Maine.

Radon comes from the rocks and soils, too, from the radioactive decay of uranium. In fact, uranium creates a large number of radioactive elements, including radium, radon, francium, polonium, and others before it becomes lead, which is stable and nonradioactive (though not something anyone would want to eat or breathe, because lead tricks the body into thinking that it is another metal such as calcium, a substance the body actually needs).

Cosmic rays at sea level come mostly from outside the solar system, from exploding stars elsewhere in the galaxy. But, at higher altitudes, say on an airplane, radiation levels are a little higher than on the ground; most of this difference is due to radiation from the Sun.

Radioactivity exists in the human body as, again, the radioactive potassium (K-40). This is the second-most significant source of radiation for most people, and there is absolutely no way to avoid it. High-potassium foods like bananas also have a little more radioactive K-40 in them. This level of radiation has extremely low risk—but a potassium deficiency can be very risky because of how potassium helps muscles (including the heart) to work properly.

Artificial Radiation

Man-made radiation sources include X-rays and other medical procedures, such as CT scans, as well as nuclear medicine. Adults (especially older adults) have many more of these procedures than children usually do, so most children receive much less medical radiation than their parents and grandparents.

Many consumer products use radioactivity as well, some deliberately and some just by coincidence. Smoke detectors use radioactive americium to help detect fires— and their very low levels of radioactivity are not dangerous. Glossy magazines are coated with clays containing K-40.

(continues)

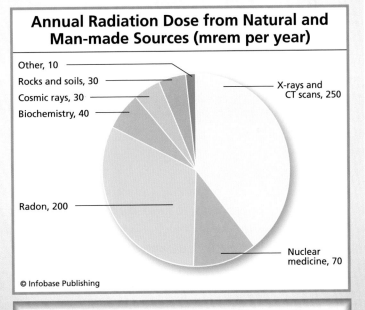

Annual Radiation Dose from Natural and Man-made Sources (mrem per year)

Other, 10

Rocks and soils, 30

Cosmic rays, 30

Biochemistry, 40

X-rays and CT scans, 250

Radon, 200

Nuclear medicine, 70

© Infobase Publishing

Figure 1.2 Radiation is everywhere, and it comes from sources that are both natural (like cosmic rays) and man-made (like medical radiation).

(continued)

In fact, bricks, concrete, cinder blocks, and other building materials also contain K-40. Some TV sets give off very low levels of X-rays (again, not in dangerous amounts), and some forms of high-quality optical glass use thorium. However, all of these radioactive elements are present in safe levels.

Of the "other" sources of radiation, the biggest is radioactive fallout from the era of atmospheric nuclear weapons testing and (more recently) from the nuclear reactor accident at Chernobyl, Ukraine. But, except for those people living near these areas, the radiation levels are low; by now, the radioactivity from these areas has spread out to low levels all around the Earth.

means that the sheet is too thin. At this point, a signal is sent to the machinery that controls the thickness of the steel, telling it to make the sheet a little thicker. Radioactive gauges are also used to control the thickness of paper, to see if bottles and cans are filled high enough, to warn that tanks are about to overflow (or to empty out), and to see if the ground is strong enough to support a building or a new road.

And this is only the beginning. Industry also uses radiation and radioactivity to inspect pipes, to make sure that airplane brake pads are in good shape, and much, much more. In fact, industry depends on radiation as much as medicine and research—and, in some cases, even more.

This book will explain where radiation comes from and how it can affect human health. It will explain how nuclear reactors work, including a natural nuclear reactor that operated on Earth over 2 billion years ago. This book will also show how radiation and radioactivity can affect the environment. It will reveal how radiation is used in medicine and in industry, and the benefits to society from the use of radiation. And, finally, the book concludes with some simple experiments—using natural sources of radiation—that can be done at home and school.

Radiation in Nature

The previous chapter discussed natural sources of radiation in the environment and how this **background radiation** is inescapable. Now it is time to talk about these sources in a little more detail. Natural radiation comes from radioactive atoms in rocks and soils, from radon, from outer space, and from within the human body. In addition, radiation comes from man-made sources, including medical sources, some consumer products, and radioactive fallout from past nuclear weapons testing.

RADIATION IN NATURE

As scientists can best determine, billions of years ago a nearby star exploded and spewed out virtually all of the elements (types of atoms), including most of the radioactive ones, that formed the Earth. Here's the rest of the story.

Radioactivity in the Earth

When the Earth first formed, its material was well mixed, or uniform, or what scientists call **homogeneous**. It was like pouring chocolate syrup into a glass of milk and stirring it up: At first, the white milk and the brown chocolate are easy to see, but, once they are thoroughly stirred, the entire glass becomes the same color—every drop of chocolate milk will look the same. The Earth during its earliest days was like that: Rocks everywhere had the same chemical composition. But today's Earth is different all over its surface: Some rocks are black, some are pink, some are grainy, and so forth. Somewhere along the line, the Earth changed—different parts started to look different. This process helps to explain why some rocks are also more radioactive than others today.

There are a lot of volcanoes on the Earth today, but there were far more in the past. A volcano is an area where molten rock from inside the Earth breaks through the surface. This much everyone knows. What is not as well known is what happens inside the molten rock, or magma, before it even erupts. From the perspective of radioactivity, the most important thing is that the magma starts to solidify even when it is deep underground. As it does this, radioactive atoms tend to stay in the remaining magma. The magma that finally reaches the surface of the Earth contains a higher concentration of radioactive atoms than did the original rock. Over time, most of the radioactive atoms that were inside the original Earth have moved into its outermost layer, known as the crust.

However, the level of radioactivity varies even within the rocks in the crust. For example, the solid black lava from Hawaii rises up directly from the mantle, which is the layer of the Earth directly below the crust. If all the radioactivity on the Earth is now located in the crust, that means there is very little of it in the mantle's rocks. So, Hawaiian rocks should have low radioactivity levels. This is, in fact, precisely what scientists have found. This is one way of proving that almost all of the Earth's radioactivity is in the crust. Also, rocks in the crust should have higher levels of radioactivity, and it may even be that the youngest rocks, the ones that have gone through the most mixing in the Earth, should have the very highest levels of radioactivity. This, again, is exactly what scientists observe when they look at different kinds of rocks. So, even though the Earth began its life as a fairly homogeneous (uniform) sphere, it has steadily become more nonuniform over time—almost as though chocolate milk separated into chocolate syrup and white milk all on its own.

Anywhere on Earth, there is always some radiation coming from the rocks. But even the soil contains radioactivity. This is because soils form from the rocks underneath. As soon as a rock forms, it begins to break down as it comes into contact with the atmosphere and experiences the effects of weather. This process is known as weathering. As it breaks down, the rock is mixed with decaying plant materials and ultimately forms soil. So, the soils come from the underlying rocks, diluted somewhat with plants, which scientists call **organic** material. In fact, the amount of radioactivity in the soils is fairly similar to what is found in the rocks, so scientists can also predict that rocks with higher levels of radioactivity will be underneath soils that also have higher levels of radioactivity. Around the Earth, the amount of radioactivity in the rocks and soils is quite variable, from very low levels (in places like Hawaii) to very high levels (in places like Ramsar, Iran, and Kerala, India).

There are three main forms of natural radioactive atoms that are found on Earth. Called **radionuclides**, these atoms are known as uranium, thorium, and potassium. These atoms have all been around since the Earth first formed, and they will all probably still be around when the Sun burns out billions of years from now. Even though radioactive potassium breaks down, or decays, into nonradioactive atoms, uranium and thorium decay to atoms that are also radioactive. These, in turn, decay to other radioactive atoms, which decay to still more radioactive atoms—this process continues through many steps until they decay into lead atoms, which are stable. Some of these other radioactive atoms, such as radium, radon, and polonium, are well known: Radium was used to make glow-in-the-dark watches and clocks; homeowners worry about radon entering basements; and a Russian dissident was poisoned and killed with polonium in 2006. On average, the radioactive elements in rocks and soils expose residents in the United States and Canada to radiation levels of 2.8 mSv (28 mrem) yearly. This is a very small amount of radiation.

Radon, which exists in just about every home, is created when uranium atoms decay toward stable lead atoms. Radon is a radioactive gas, chemically similar to the atoms helium and argon. Radon is heavier than air, so it will collect in low places, like basements. Radon levels tend to be higher in areas that have more uranium in the

Uranium 238 (U238) Radioactive Decay Chain

	Nuclide	Half-life
	uranium—238	4.5×10^9 years
	thorium—234	24.5 days
	protactinium—234	1.14 minutes
	uranium—234	2.33×10^5 years
	thorium—230	8.3×10^4 years
	radium—226	1,590 years
	radon—222	3.825 days
	polonium—218	3.05 minutes
	lead—214	26.8 minutes
	bismuth—214	19.7 minutes
	polonium—214	1.5×10^{-4} seconds
	lead—210	22 years
	bismuth—210	5 days
	polonium—210	140 days
	lead—206	stable

Figure 2.1 Types of radiation and half-lives of different nuclides

rocks and soil, so Hawaii (and other places with a lot of basalt, which forms when black lava solidifies) has lower levels of radon than many of the New England states. On average, people in the United States and Canada get about 2 mSv (200 mrem) each year from radon, but, as with radiation from the rocks and soils, radon concentrations also change quite a bit from place to place.

Many new homes are sealed pretty tightly to save energy. Unfortunately, this also traps radon inside the homes, and there has been some concern that this might expose residents to dangerous levels of radiation. Luckily, radon levels in most homes are low, and there is no need to worry in those homes—even for people who sleep in the basement. In some homes, radon levels are high enough to be worrisome. In most of these, simply sealing cracks in the floor and painting the floor and walls with a tough paint will help reduce radon to safe levels.

Another interesting fact about radon is that it can even give doses of radiation to people who smoke cigarettes. Radon, when it decays, forms radioactive **nuclides** of lead, bismuth, and polonium, which settle out of the air onto the large tobacco leaves. When a person smokes the tobacco, these nuclides enter the lungs. It is estimated that a person who smokes a pack of cigarettes each day will deliver tens of milliSieverts (a few thousand mrem) a year to his or her lungs. Over a lifetime of smoking, this is enough radiation to create a fairly high risk of developing cancer. It is also interesting to note that one of these radionuclides—polonium-210—is the same that was used to poison the Russian dissident Alexander Litvinenko in late 2006, although he was given much higher quantities of the polonium.

Radiation from Space

Although people receive most natural radiation from the Earth, some radiation comes from space. Some of it comes from the Sun, but a lot comes from cosmic rays that originate from outside the solar system: These are called galactic cosmic rays (GCRs). Believe it or not, at sea level, there is more radiation dose from GCRs than from the Sun, even though the GCRs may have traveled thousands or millions of light years before reaching the Earth. The fact is that cosmic rays from the sun have too little energy to penetrate all the way through the atmosphere to reach the Earth's surface—but the much higher-energy GCRs possess enough "oomph" to make it all the way through the atmosphere. So, at sea level, most of the cosmic radiation dose to humans comes from outside the solar system . . . or even from a galaxy far, far away! On Earth, the atmosphere provides most of the protection against cosmic radiation—every square centimeter of the Earth's sur-face has over 2.2 pounds (1 kilogram) of air reaching up to outer space. This is equivalent to a column of water 33 feet (10 meters) deep—that is a lot of shielding. It also means that cosmic radia-tion dose increases with elevation—whether they are in the moun-tains or in an aircraft, people receive a slightly higher radiation dose. The other factor that protects people from cosmic radiation is the Earth's magnetic field. Magnetic fields deflect anything with an electrical charge, and most cosmic rays are charged particles. So Earth's magnetic field pushes the cosmic rays away from the Earth. A stronger magnetic field causes a larger deflection, and the Earth's magnetic field is strongest over the equator. Because of this, cosmic radiation dose is somewhat lower at the equator than it is at the north and south poles. However, this difference is not very large—only about 15 to 20% from pole to equator—so even if the Earth's magnetic field disappears entirely, the radiation dose will not increase to dangerous levels. But this is not surprising. After all, the Earth's magnetic field has vanished and reestablished itself many times over the history of life on the planet, and it has never caused a mass extinction. So scientists can be fairly certain that the loss of the Earth's magnetic field will not be fatal to humans or to other species. All in all, at sea level, cosmic radiation exposes peo-ple to about 0.27 mSv (27 mrem) each year when averaged across the United States and Canada. That is about equal to the dose from three chest X-rays.

Because astronauts travel outside of the Earth's atmosphere (and sometimes beyond the Earth's magnetic field, as happened when as-tronauts went to the Moon and will happen again if humankind re-turns to the Moon and goes to Mars), they receive a lot more radia-tion exposure than the rest of the human population. If there is a solar

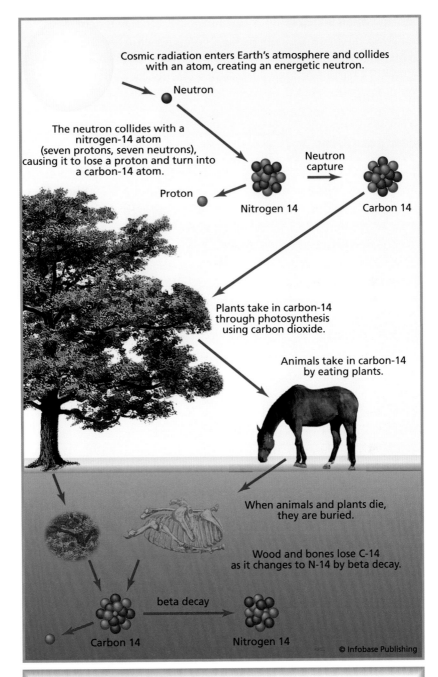

Figure 2.2 When cosmic radiation enters the Earth's atmosphere it undergoes a series of reactions.

"storm" when a spaceship is beyond the Earth's magnetic field, the radiation dose can actually be high enough to hurt or kill the astronauts. This is why many of the plans for spaceships traveling to Mars include radiation shielding to protect the astronauts during a large solar storm.

Radioactivity in the Human Body

In addition to the radiation coming from the Earth and the cosmos, every human body contains radioactivity: About 1/100th of 1% of potassium is radioactive potassium-40 (K-40). This exposes people to an additional 0.35 to 0.37 mSv (35 to 37 mrem) each year.

That does not account, however, for the entire amount of **internal radioactivity** found in people. Radioactive nuclides of hydrogen and carbon (H-3, also called tritium, and carbon-14) are produced when cosmic rays strike atoms in the atmosphere. These nuclides are spread throughout the Earth and are incorporated into every living organism on the planet—including all people and the food they eat. And then there is dust and dirt—everyone ingests a little bit of these and the radionuclides they contain—as part of meals, or simply by breathing. There is always some dust in the air, and everyone breathes it into their lungs. Dust also settles onto plants and fruits and, in turn, is eaten by people when they do not wash the food beforehand. The uranium, thorium, and radium in the dust will enter the bones, although at tiny levels that are not dangerous. All in all, these other internal sources of radioactivity expose humans to another 0.03 to 0.05 mSv (3 to 5 mrem) each year, for a total of .4 mSv (40 mrem) from all sources of radioactivity in the human body—the equivalent of about four chest X-rays. This amount is relatively constant for all people.When this is all added together, people in the United States and Canada are exposed to about 2.95 mSv (295 mrem) each year from natural sources. This level of exposure is lower in some places, and can be much higher in others. In fact, in some other places around the world, such as parts of Brazil, China, India, and Iran, people can be exposed to 20 mSv (2,000 mrem) each year, or more. This is equivalent to about 200 dental X-rays.

MAN-MADE BACKGROUND RADIATION

People are also exposed to radiation from man-made sources, although most do not normally receive as much radiation from these sources as they do from nature. Artificial sources of radiation include medical radiation, consumer products, radioactive fallout from past nuclear weapons testing, nuclear power, and more.

Medical Radiation

The biggest source of artificial radiation is medicine. Dental X-rays, medical X-rays, CT scans, PET scans, nuclear medicine, and radiation oncology (which uses radiation to treat cancer) will all expose the patient to some level of radiation. Some of these, such as X-rays, expose the patient to a low level of radiation—usually only a few tenths to a few mSv (a few tens to a few hundred mrem) for each of these procedures. This relatively low level of radiation exposure means that these procedures are safe for the patient—this is why doctors and dentists do not worry about having patients undergo these X-rays. CT scans expose the patient to more radiation, up to several tens of mSv (several thousand mrem) each. A single CT scan, or even a few CT scans, will not put a patient at risk from the radiation, especially not when a physician thinks that these scans are necessary. However, many people decide, without a doctor's advice, to have a CT scan done—sometimes many of them. While this can sometimes help a patient to find problems that they would not otherwise have been aware of, most of the time it simply exposes the patient to radiation without any real medical benefit.

Nuclear medicine procedures involve injecting radioactive substances into a patient to help diagnose or treat disease. Injecting the radioactivity into the patient also exposes the person to radiation, but the risk from the radiation is much lower than the risk from having an undiagnosed disease.

All told, on average, people in the United States receive about 3.3 mSv (330 mrem) each year from medical procedures, although some (such as those who have many CT scans or receive cancer therapy) receive much more than this. Radiation from medical procedures will be discussed more in Chapter 7.

Consumer Products

There are some products that people can buy that are radioactive. In fact, many consumer products have some level of radioactivity in them. Glossy magazines, for example, get their gloss from a clay that

Nature's Nuclear Reactor in Gabon, Africa

On December 2, 1942, Enrico Fermi and his group of scientists, working underneath some old unused stands of a football stadium, created Chicago Pile 1, the first man-made nuclear reactor. Today, nuclear reactors are taken for granted—in fact, the United States has about 100 operating nuclear reactors, and there are about 500 worldwide. Nuclear reactors are seen by many as a triumph of human ingenuity and engineering design, even if many also feel that they are dangerous (Chapter 4 will discuss this issue in more detail). What Fermi did not know—in fact, what nobody in the world knew until 1972—was that Chicago Pile 1 was not the first nuclear reactor in the history of the Earth after all. In fact, nature had beaten Fermi by over a billion years.

In 1972, the French government was mining for nuclear reactor fuel from a massive uranium ore deposit in Gabon, Africa. As they analyzed the uranium, they discovered some irregularities that could only mean one thing—that the uranium had been involved in **nuclear fission** reactions, in which the cores of atoms, or **nuclei**, were being split apart. This was impossible, they thought. But then a further study of the uranium deposit showed that, just by accident, the uranium had been arranged in the rocks in a way that made it possible—nearly 2 billion years ago—to actually sustain a **chain reaction** in which the split, or fission, of some nuclei would trigger the splitting of other nuclei. Later experiments and tests confirmed that the uranium really contains some potassium (including radioactive potassium-40). So, these magazines actually give off a little radiation—but not nearly enough to be a cause for worry.

Smoke detectors also contain a little radiation, which helps them to detect the smoke particles. But, again, this amount is so low that

had collected in such a way that it could operate for over 100,000 years as a natural nuclear reactor. What made the discovery even more surprising was that almost all of the radioactive waste was still there.

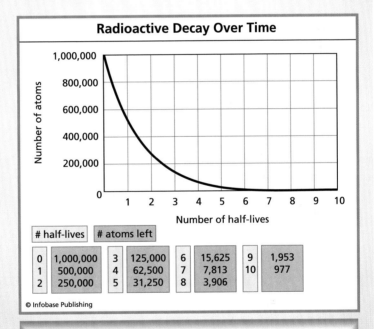

Radioactive Decay Over Time

# half-lives	# atoms left						
0	1,000,000	3	125,000	6	15,625	9	1,953
1	500,000	4	62,500	7	7,813	10	977
2	250,000	5	31,250	8	3,906		

© Infobase Publishing

Figure 2.3 Over the course of each half-life of a radioactive element, the total number of atoms in a sample decreases by half as the element decays into a different element. In this example, after one half-life, only 500,000 of the original 1,000,000 atoms are left. Of these remaining 500,000, only half, or 250,000 atoms, remain after the second half-life. This repeats until the sample has completely decayed.

it is not a risk; people are at far more risk from not having smoke detectors. Smoke detectors really do save lives and having them in homes is important.

There are other products that also expose individuals to low levels of radiation: Salt substitutes have potassium, some forms of glass contain either uranium or thorium, some jewelry contains small quantities of uranium, and so forth. All in all, people receive about 0.1 mSv (10 mrem) each year from these consumer products, which is not very much and is equivalent to about one chest X-ray.

Other Sources of Radiation

Aside from the major sources of radiation, minor sources of radiation account for about another 0.02 mSv (2 mrem) each year. These include things like radioactive fallout from nuclear weapons that were tested in the 1950s and 1960s, as well as small levels of fallout from the nuclear reactor accident at Chernobyl. Nuclear power plants also expose nearby residents to very low levels of radiation, as do **radioactive waste** shipments. But, again, all of these other sources of radiation only come out to about 0.02 mSv (2 mrem) each year on average.

Added together, about 3.3 mSv (330 mrem) each year comes from man-made sources of radiation, and about 3.6 mSv (360 mrem) each year comes from all sources of background radiation. This is radiation that no one can escape, but this level of radiation exposure seems to be safe.

HALF-LIFE AND RADIOACTIVE DATING

Radioactive atoms give off energy in the form of radiation. This is called radioactive decay. Each kind of radioactive atom, or nuclide, decays at a particular rate, or speed, called the **half-life**. More accurately, for any given nuclide, the half-life is the amount of time that it takes for one-half of a group of them to decay. After one half-life, one-half of the original atoms are gone and one-half remain. After a second half-life, one-half of those remaining atoms decay, so one-quarter of the original radioactive atoms remain. After another half-life, one-eighth of the original radioactive atoms are still there, and so forth.

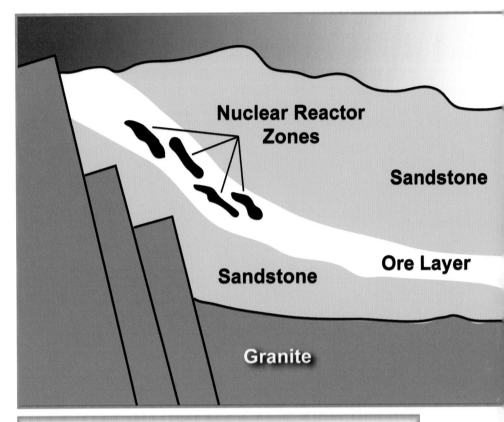

Figure 2.4   This schematic describes the structure of the natural nuclear reactor found at the Oklo uranium mine in Gabon, Africa.

Radioactive decay can be used to measure the ages of rocks and archeological artifacts. Say, for example, a rock contains a certain amount of a radioactive atom that has a half-life of 10 million years. Analyzing the rock can actually reveal the number of radioactive atoms, as well as the number of the "**daughter**" **nuclides**, which are those atoms created by the decay of the original "**parent**" radioactive **nuclides** in the sample. If the sample contains the same number of each atom, that means one-half of the original atoms have decayed away, so the rock must be one half-life old—10 million years. However, if the sample contains three daughter atoms for every radioactive atom, then the rock is 20 million

	Table 2.1 Some Naturally Radioactive Nuclides and Their Properties			
Nuclide	Half-life	Where it is found	Where it comes from	What it is used for
Rb-87	49 billion years	Rocks	Primordial (from the earliest days of the Earth)	Determining the age of rocks and other geological samples (geologic dating)
Th-232	14 billion years	Rocks and soils	Primordial	Many products (high-quality glass, welding rods, jet turbine blades, etc.)
U-238	4.5 billion years	Rocks and soils	Primordial	Tank armor, anti-tank munitions
K-40	1.3 billion years	Rocks, soils, living organisms	Primordial	Geologic dating
U-235	700 million years	Rocks and soils	Primordial	Nuclear reactor fuel, nuclear weapons
Be-10	1.5 million years	Atmosphere, rocks	Cosmic rays	Geologic dating
C-14	5,730 years	Atmosphere, all living things	Cosmic ray interactions	Determining the age of archeological artifacts (carbon dating)
Ra-226	1,600 years	Rocks and soils	U-238 decay	Self-luminous products
H-3	12.3 years	Atmosphere, all living things	Cosmic rays	Research, nuclear weapons
Po-210	138 days	Rocks and soils	U-238 decay	Static eliminators
Rn-222	3.8 days	Air	U-238 decay	No use

years old (after 2 half-lives, there are one-quarter of the original atoms and three-quarters of the daughter atoms, for a ratio of 3 to 1). So, the number of parent and daughter nuclides and the number of half-lives can reveal how old a rock is.

Radiation and Health

Radiation turned a normal man into the Incredible Hulk. Cosmic radiation turned four astronauts into the Fantastic Four. In the original Spiderman, the bite from a radioactive spider turned a normal person into Spiderman, and radiation also turned a lizard into Godzilla and ordinary ants into monster ants in the movie *Them*. Of course, none of these stories are real. In real life, radiation cannot do any of these things.

In real life, radiation can affect human health. However, these effects are not always clear. At high doses, radiation can cause skin burns, make people vomit, and even cause death. At doses that are lower, although still much higher than most humans are normally exposed to, radiation can cause cancer. At those lower doses that people receive from nature and from medical radiation, it is not exactly certain how radiation affects human health, if it has any effects at all. But scientists do have a lot of information on these questions, and this chapter will explain what scientists do know, as well as some of the things that scientists do not yet fully understand.

RADIATION AND CELLS

What happens when radiation enters a human cell? First, it is important to remember that a cell is made up of different parts. Like a castle, the cell is protected by a wall, or membrane, that shields it from many things in the outside world. Inside the membrane, there is the cell nucleus, a round blob that acts as the command center of the cell.

Inside the nucleus are x-shaped objects. They are called chromosomes, what scientists call the "genetic material of the cell." Humans have 23 pairs of chromosomes in each cell, totaling 46 chromosomes in all. Together, the 46 chromosomes in any cell contain *all* the instructions for the entire body. Each chromosome, in turn, is made up of a large molecule called **DNA**. DNA looks like a ladder that has been twisted in a spiral to form a shape called a "double helix." The DNA in the cell's largest chromosome has almost 250 million rungs. Many segments of the DNA ladders contain *genes* that provide instructions for making the proteins in the human body. When something, including radiation, damages these genes, they can go haywire and create cancer.

How exactly does radiation cause this damage? When scientists look through an electron microscope that has been adjusted to the highest magnification, they see that the building blocks of everything in the cell are atoms and molecules. Many of these molecules are much smaller than DNA and they have many different shapes. In addition to cells, atoms also have something called a *nucleus*, but the *atomic* nucleus is a much smaller and (usually) round core made of positively charged particles. Just as cells are surrounded by a membrane, atoms and molecules are surrounded by negatively charged electrons that whiz around them.

The full scientific term for radiation is **ionizing radiation**. When radiation hits an atom or molecule in the cell, it kicks out one of the cell's electrons, turning that atom or molecule into a positively charged ion. At the same time that the radiation hits that atom or molecule, it deposits that energy to one of the electrons that surrounds it. When the radiation has enough energy to let the electron escape, it is considered "ionizing radiation," as it has enough energy to turn that atom or molecule into an ion.

An electron around an atomic nucleus can be imagined as a small satellite orbiting the Earth. If the electron receives a little energy, it will momentarily be bumped to a higher-energy state, or orbit, but it will stay with the atomic nucleus. If it receives enough energy, the electron will escape from the nucleus entirely, like a satellite being knocked out of orbit. This process is called *ionization,* and it creates an ion pair—a negatively charged electron plus the rest of the atom, which is now positively charged. Atoms and molecules are normally neutral with no net electrical charge—they have as many positive charges (protons) as they do negative charges (electrons). An ion is any atom or molecule with an electrical charge, which usually happens when an electron is removed (giving a net positive charge) or when an extra electron is added (giving a net negative charge).

When ionizing radiation creates an ion pair in cells, the ion pairs can combine with atoms, molecules, or other ion pairs to form chemicals called *free radicals.* Free radicals are molecules that are very, very active. They can attack the cell's basic genetic material, the DNA, causing damage—or mutations—to the DNA, which is potentially dangerous. However, free radicals can be created by other things besides radiation, such as chemicals that enter the body, or even natural processes in the cells. Free radicals can damage cells in the same way no matter how they are created. So, radiation has no unique, special "powers" to harm an individual cell. It creates free radicals that can damage the cell in the same ways as free radicals that are created from other processes.

When a cell's DNA is damaged, it is most likely that the cell will repair the damage and that there will be no problems at all. This is what happens most of the time—for example, when ultraviolet rays from the sun create pairs of ions (charged particles) in the skin. If the damage is repaired correctly (though it is always possible to make a mistake), then the damage might not have any effect at all; in fact, most DNA damage and most mutations have no impact on the cell because there are many parts of the DNA that are not used by most cells. This is sort of like the instructions for a portable audio player that are printed in many languages—if there is a page missing from the Japanese instructions or if someone scribbles on the German instructions, it will not make a difference to someone who needs only the English instructions.

However, on very rare occasions, the DNA damage will be in an important part of the genome: the set of full genetic instructions contained in the cell. If the cell can function normally despite this damage, then there are no repercussions—it cannot harm the rest of the organism. Still, it is possible that the radiation might cause cancer.

THE RISK OF CANCER

DNA and the instructions it carries exert tight controls over most cells concerning when and why they will divide to form new cells. But sometimes damage to a cell's DNA can cause the cell to divide uncontrollably; when this happens, the cells can form a mass—a tumor—that can endanger a person's life. This is what cancer is. Radiation can cause the sort of DNA damage that can lead to cancer. The question is how much radiation does it take to cause cancer? What is the risk from a small amount of radiation exposure? These are among the biggest questions, so far unanswered, in radiation biology. Because cancer is a frightening disease, and because scientists do not usually monitor the (usually very small) doses of invisible radiation that enter the body, many people are scared of radiation.

Some scientists think that any exposure to radiation might be potentially dangerous, and that the danger is directly proportional to the amount of radiation that a person receives. According to this hypothesis, someone who is exposed to 0.02 Sv (2 rem) of radiation will have double the risk of cancer as someone exposed to 0.01 Sv (1 rem). These scientists also think that any level of radiation exposure is potentially risky, even if that risk is very, very low for very low levels of radiation exposure.

Other scientists disagree with this hypothesis; they think that below a certain level of exposure—a threshold—there is actually no risk at all of developing cancer from low levels of radiation. These scientists point out that there is a threshold for danger with almost everything. For example, swallowing a microscopic amount of lead will not cause lead poisoning. That occurs only when a larger amount of lead is ingested by the body.

Many scientists think that this idea of a threshold applies to radiation—that there might be a level of radiation exposure that does not have any potential danger. This is not unheard of; in fact, most dangerous substances have some point at which that danger is no longer present. The scientists who believe that there might be such a threshold think that it might occur when someone is exposed—all at one time—to about 0.1 or 0.2 Sv (10 or 20 rem) of radiation. This is about 40 times the average natural radiation exposure a person receives in North America over a single *year*. And even if this is true, such individuals would not always get cancer—though the risk of getting it would be increased.

There are other scientists who will go even further and say that low levels of radiation might even be good for us, that a little bit of radiation might help us avoid getting cancer—this is called *hormesis*. Although this idea sounds crazy, there are many similar examples of this idea: People with heart problems may take a small aspirin every day to stay healthy, but taking an entire bottle all at once can be dangerous. And there are many things in vitamins that, in small quantities, are necessary for health but in large quantities become dangerous. For example, small quantities of selenium are necessary for a person's health, but high levels of this substance are dangerously toxic. High levels of some vitamins are also dangerous, even though normal levels are necessary for health. Therefore, some scientists think that radiation may also provide health benefits at low levels of exposure, even if high levels of exposure are known to be harmful.

When people hear that scientists are not certain about something, many think that the next step is to run another test or to analyze the data further. Unfortunately, much scientific data is "noisy"; this means that the measurements vary slightly from experiment to experiment. Some studies, for example, show that cancer rates are a little higher as radiation dose increases, while other studies show that cancer risk drops a little bit, and still other studies show that there is no difference at all. These are not bad studies—it is just that, in the real world, not everything is perfectly clear. There is always some error in the data, and it is not always easy to figure out the exact answer.

For example, in the United States, about 2% of people have naturally red hair—about 2 people out of every 100. So say a scientist decides to go around town to count redheaded people by counting groups of 100. In one group, there might only be 1 redhead, while, in the next group, there might be 4. Other groups might have 1, 1, 6, 3, 0, 1, 3, and 0. So out of 10 groups, there would be no groups with the average number of redheads, 4 groups with a higher number than average, and 6 groups with less than average numbers of redheads. In other words, no single group would have the "right" number of redheads in it. Furthermore, if the scientist studied just the groups that contain only 1 or 0 redheads in them, he might conclude that the redheads in the United States made up only 0.67% of the population, while if he studied only the groups with higher numbers of redheads, he might think that the U.S. population had 4% redheads. Of

Radiation Units

Scientists measure things in terms of units. Radiation and radiation dose are measured in the same way. Scientists use units to tell us how much radioactivity there is, how much radiation dose people are exposed to, and how much damage exposure might do to the body.

Radioactivity units: the Becquerel (Bq) and the Curie (Ci)

One Bq is the amount of any radioactive material that produces 1 radioactive decay every second. One mega-Bq (MBq) of material undergoes 1 million decays per second, and 1 billion Bq (GBq) has a decay rate of 1 billion decays every second.

One curie (Ci) gives a decay rate of 37 billion decays every second, so 1 Ci = 37 GBq.

Radiation dose units: the Gray (Gy) and Rad (R), and the Sievert (Sv) and rem

The gray (Gy) and rad units measure the amount of radiation energy that is deposited in the body: 1 Gy = 100 rad.

In addition, some types of radiation are more damaging to DNA than others—for example, alpha radiation damages DNA more than beta and gamma radiation. So 1 rad of alpha radiation is more likely to cause cancer than 1 rad of beta or gamma radiation. These differences are reflected in the "quality factor" for each kind of radiation. The Sievert (Sv) and rem units describe the biological damage done by radiation when it is absorbed in the body. The number of Sv (or rem) a person receives is equal to the number of **Grays** (or rads) times the quality factor for the radiation. For example, alpha radiation has a quality factor of 20, so 1 gray of alpha radiation is equivalent to 20 Sieverts.

course, both of these averages are wrong—just as it would be wrong to look at only a few cancer studies and use those to conclude that low levels of radiation were either harmful or beneficial.

The problem with all of these radiation studies is that there are simply too few of them, and the deviation from the average is simply too small to say for sure whether or not there is any real difference. This is why scientists often call for more studies of a particular topic—more studies usually (but not always) help scientists zero in on the accurate answers.

What scientists can say for sure is that, even with all of the problems mentioned above, low levels of radiation exposure (what most radiation workers are exposed to during their careers) present the same likelihood of causing cancer as a person's likelihood of being in a traffic accident—maybe even lower.

HIGH DOSES OF RADIATION

People have sometimes been exposed to very high doses of radiation, sometimes in accidents, and also in other ways, as when nuclear weapons were dropped on Hiroshima and Nagasaki at the end of World War II. Even though scientists are not always sure about what the risks are from low doses of radiation, they are very sure about what happens when people are exposed to very high radiation levels. Because the effects are so much greater, they are easier to see.

At higher doses of radiation, blood cells start to become affected. In particular, the white blood cells—the cells that fight infections in the body—are the most affected, along with the organs that make the white blood cells. Doctors have reported that a radiation dose of 0.25 Sv (25 rem) or higher will cause the number of white blood cells to start dropping. If someone is exposed to 1 Sv (100 rem) at one time—about 400 times what the average North American receives in a year—they might start to feel sick; they will feel like vomiting and they might not be able to get out of bed in the morning. But neither they nor their doctors might see that this is due to radiation because the flu or a bad cold can cause the same symptoms.

The higher the radiation dose, the sicker a person feels. By the time they get to a dose of 4 or 5 Sv (400 or 500 rem)—2,000 times the typical yearly exposure—a person might even die from radiation

How DNA Works

DNA is the genetic code—it tells cells how to make the chemicals that help them to function properly, and it also carries the instructions to help cells work. But how does DNA do all of this?

The DNA molecule is shaped like a twisted ladder. Each rung of this ladder has a specific chemical on each side, as shown in Figure 3.1. These chemicals are adenine, thymine, guanine, and cytosine (abbreviated A, T, G, and C, respectively). They are always paired up in a particular way so that A is always opposite T, and G is always matched with C. These letters are arranged in a particular order that makes a set of instructions that tell cells how to make certain compounds or how to use those compounds—in a sense, DNA is like a big book of coded instructions.

It should be possible to decode these instructions—after all, everything in books is a set of code. For example, the word *dog* is simply a set of letters: *d, o,* and *g.* If these letters are rearranged as *god,* it means something different, while if they are rearranged as *ogd,* it becomes meaningless. These three letters, in and of themselves, have no meaning. Their meaning comes from deciphering the code, so that the word *dog* provides an image of an animal that normally lives with people, likes to play "fetch," and licks people's faces, and so forth. Similarly, the DNA bases have no meaning in and of themselves, but cells can give them meaning (for example, by "reading" the sequence "TGG" as the amino acid tryptophan), just as people give meaning to the words that they read.

Proteins are molecules that help make the body work. Insulin, for example, is a protein that helps the body use sugar for energy. Proteins are built of amino acids—these are sort of like building blocks or Lego blocks. There are over 20 kinds of amino acids, and the order that they are

(continues)

DNA Structure

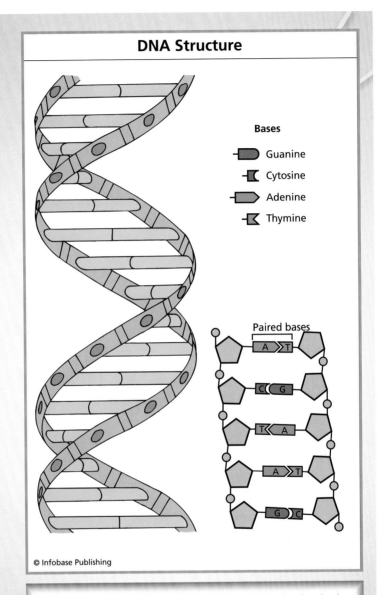

Figure 3.1 The DNA molecule is a double helix that looks like a twisted ladder. The steps of the ladder are made up of small molecules called bases. DNA's four bases are adenine, thymine, guanine, and cytosine, and their sequence determines the genetic code.

(continued)

put together helps to make proteins function correctly. In a way, it is like building a model airplane—the right pieces have to go together in the correct order for it to work properly. Each amino acid has a three-letter code. For example, the amino acid methionine has the code ATG. As the DNA is "read," and if the sequence ATG is found, it tells the cell to put methionine in that location. Combined with all of the other sets of letters in the DNA, this will tell the cell to make, for example, insulin. If one of these letters is changed, then the DNA will tell the cell to put in the wrong amino acid, and this can change the protein to something that might not work as well. This is called a *mutation*.

Mutations can cause problems like diseases. But there are many things that mutations cannot cause. For example, a mutation will not suddenly change the way a person looks. So a normal person will not turn into the Hulk because of radiation exposure, and a lizard cannot turn into Godzilla.

poisoning. However, at this level of exposure, a person is also getting sick from disease because the white blood cells affected first by the radiation are the same cells that help to fight germs, and without these cells, a person might die from pneumonia or some other sickness. If doctors can treat the illness, then these patients' lives can be saved.

At even higher radiation doses, people start to feel even worse. By the time their dose is 8 Sv (800 rem)—over 3,000 times the average yearly exposure—not even the best medical treatment can help them. Above 8 Sv (800 rem), most of those exposed will probably die from radiation sickness. But it is important to remember that this is a lot of radiation exposure—even after the accident at the Chernobyl nuclear power plant (which spread radioactivity across almost half of the Earth), only about 20 to 25 people were exposed to such a high dose of radiation.

Outside of the Chernobyl accident and the atomic bombs, very few people have ever been exposed to such a high radiation dose. In fact, outside of some sort of accident, almost nobody is ever exposed to even 0.1 Sv (10 rem), let alone those greater amounts that can cause radiation sickness.

Radiation can affect human cells by causing ionization in the atoms or molecules in the body. This can cause the formation of free radicals that can affect human DNA. DNA damage, in turn, can lead to cancer, and if the radiation dose is high enough, it can cause radiation sickness and even death. However, such high levels of exposure have been very, very rare.

Nuclear Energy

Flip a light switch and a room lights up. Press the button on a computer, and the screen lights up. Plug a cell phone into a wall outlet and the battery recharges. Turn on a stereo and it plays music. And then there are toasters, blenders, clock radios, stoves, ovens, and televisions. Society runs on electricity, and it is hard to find anything in everyday life that does not use it in some way, even in ways people do not think about. The wood in furniture, for example, is probably cut from logs using electric-powered saws. Cars are manufactured of steel welded together with electric arcs, and large parts of them are assembled by electric robots. People depend on electricity, and almost every aspect of modern life depends to a greater or lesser extent on electricity.

So, what does electricity have to do with radiation? In the United States, one watt out of every five—20% of the nation's electricity—is generated at one of about 100 nuclear power plants. Worldwide, about 16% of global electricity comes from nuclear power generated by over 400 nuclear reactors. And this percentage is only going to grow in the coming years. In fact, nuclear energy appears to be one of the only options available to help meet the developing world's growing power needs without adding more greenhouse gases to the atmosphere.

A major obstacle to the wider development of nuclear energy is the fact that nuclear energy scares many people: Will a nuclear reactor blow up like a nuclear bomb? Will a nuclear reactor accident—like Chernobyl or Three Mile Island—hurt families living nearby? Will radioactive waste from nuclear reactors leak? Are the benefits of nuclear energy worth the apparent dangers? The reality is that both sides in this debate are right in some ways and wrong in others.

This chapter will first show how nuclear reactors work. It will also describe nuclear reactor accidents and what actually happened during some accidents—including the amount of radiation that people were exposed to and its effects on the environment. Finally, nuclear energy will be compared to other forms of energy to see how they stack up against each other. This chapter will also cover radioactive waste and its **disposal**.

HOW NUCLEAR REACTORS WORK

Uranium is a big atom, one of the heaviest and largest atoms in the natural world. Teeming with 92 protons and well over 100 neutrons, uranium is so big that it can barely hold itself together. Give it a small "tap" by hitting it with a neutron from the outside world and it will fall apart, or *fission*, and the pieces of the atom (called fission fragments) will fly apart at a high speed.

A nuclear reactor uses uranium for fuel. The fuel is kept in a thick, metal-lined container known as the **reactor core**. Instead of plain uranium, the reactor core uses a specially enriched version that contains a high concentration of uranium-235 (U-235) in addition to the more common uranium-238 (U-238). U-235 is an **isotope** that contains 92 protons and 143 neutrons. U-238 contains three more neutrons, for a total of 146. Unlike other known forms of uranium, only U-235 naturally breaks apart, or fissions, when hit by a slow-moving neutron, which is why it is so valued in a nuclear reactor.

The uranium fission releases a lot of energy in a reactor and sends lots of neutrons flying around in the process. Long **control rods** absorb the neutrons being released in the nuclear reactor. Inserting more control rods into the reactor core absorbs more neutrons and slows down the process.

Nuclear fission can release so much energy that it can heat up the thick metal walls surrounding the reactor core, even to the point

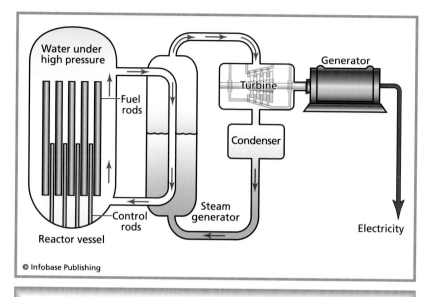

© Infobase Publishing

Figure 4.1 At a nuclear power plant, nuclear fuel heats up water to produce steam, which turns a turbine that powers an electrical generator. The steam is condensed back into water and is recycled through the plant.

of melting. To prevent melting, a large and complicated system of pipes and pumps forces water through the reactor core to remove the heat. This hot water is then used to make steam, which turns a turbine (sort of like how wind causes a windmill to spin) to operate an electrical generator. This is shown in Figure 4.1.

NUCLEAR REACTOR ACCIDENTS

January 3, 1961, 9:01 P.M.: Three military personnel powered up the Army's SL-1 experimental nuclear reactor plant. The SL-1 was designed to provide power to Army units based in the Arctic Circle. This small reactor, located at a national laboratory in Idaho, was a test facility, and on this date, the unit was being started up after being shut down for the holidays. A control rod was inserted into the reactor core to help control the power level. To start up the reactor, the operators would have to pull this rod out of the core. For some reason, one of the operators decided to pull the main control rod by hand while standing on top of the reactor. He made the mistake of pulling the rod too quickly, causing reactor power to rise quickly— too quickly, it turned out, for the water to carry the heat away safely. In a matter of moments, the water turned to steam and the steam exploded, blowing apart the reactor core. When the emergency responders reached the reactor, the interior of the reactor building was so radioactive that the responders could spend only a short time inside. All three operators had received a fatal radiation dose. This was the first fatal accident at any nuclear power plant in the United States, and even after nearly 50 years, some aspects of the incident remain a mystery.

Eighteen years later, on March 28, 1979, operators at the Three Mile Island nuclear power plant in Pennsylvania noticed some unusual instrument readings, including high radiation levels near the reactor vessel. The operators became confused, and they made a number of mistakes. Before they could determine the correct course of action, much of the nuclear fuel had melted and the reactor core was destroyed. Some radioactivity was released to the environment, and many of the local residents decided to evacuate the area. However, nobody was killed, or even injured—and in the time since, there is no evidence that anybody has been hurt or made sick from this accident.

There have been other nuclear reactor accidents in the United States, but no incidents as serious as these two, and, aside from the SL-1 accident, none have been fatal. Other countries have had nuclear reactor accidents, too, some of which have been fatal. The worst nuclear power plant accident in history happened on April 26, 1986, when the Chernobyl nuclear power plant had a catastrophic accident that not only destroyed the nuclear reactor, but also killed 31 people at the time, and may kill up to several thousand more over the decades following. In fact, as of 2006, the World Health Organization confirmed a maximum of 56 deaths from Chernobyl and estimated that up to 10,000 people may eventually die of radiation-induced cancer from Chernobyl. However, because of the very large number of people who were exposed to radiation from Chernobyl, and because of the large numbers of expected cancers from other causes among all of these people, it may never be possible to determine exactly which deaths were the result of this accident.

Figure 4.2 The Chernobyl nuclear power plant, located in what is now the Ukraine, was the site of the worst nuclear power accident ever. Here, an aerial shot shows the demolished reactor after the accident.

The Chernobyl accident was the worst of its kind: It released more radioactivity and caused more deaths than any other. But it is also unlikely that any future nuclear reactor accident will cause so much harm again. This is because Chernobyl-style nuclear reactor plants had certain problems with their design that allowed this sort of an accident to occur. Other nuclear reactors are encased within thick concrete walls to contain the radioactivity in the event of an accident. Chernobyl was enclosed only by a flimsy building. Simply adding a thick, concrete containment structure would have prevented the release of so much radioactivity. It could have reduced the number of deaths in the days and weeks after the accident, and certainly would have reduced the number of possible cancer deaths in the long run. All nuclear reactors built in the United States, Europe, Canada, and Japan have this thick concrete containment building, and, with the exception of the remaining Chernobyl-style nuclear reactors, no currently operating nuclear reactors are housed in such a flimsy structure. With luck, there will never again be a nuclear reactor accident that will release so much radioactivity into the environment, or that will cause so many deaths.

SOME COMPARISONS

Society needs energy to keep running. At first, people simply burned wood or coal, and then started to burn oil about a century ago. Eventually, people realized that this was causing problems due to air pollution—the smoke was hurting the environment and harming people's health. People started looking for ways to make the burning of fuels less polluting, and also for forms of energy that might not require burning fuels at all.

One of the answers seemed to be nuclear energy, but people were concerned about releasing radioactivity into the environment. They also thought that solar energy—similar to a solar-powered watch or solar-powered calculator—might be a better way to produce power. And people have also used water power, wind power, and geothermal energy. Each of these sources has some advantages—for example, most of them do not produce any air pollution at all—but each one of them has some disadvantages as well.

The biggest problem with wind power, solar energy, geothermal energy, and hydroelectric power is that they will only work in certain areas. For example, solar energy is not reliable where it is always cloudy, and hydroelectric power can only be used near rivers. Many of these alternatives only produce power during certain parts of the day—in the case of solar panels, for example, during daylight. So even though these are attractive sources of energy, they can only help those who live in favorable areas. Because of these problems, the world still gets most of its energy from burning fuel—usually coal, oil, or natural gas.

The biggest concern about nuclear energy is that it can release radioactivity into the environment. Some of this release is intended as a part of normal nuclear reactor plant operations; but sometimes releases happen accidentally. In addition, because radiation can cause cancer, many are concerned that living too close to a nuclear reactor can be dangerous to their health.

Most people now also realize that burning oil and natural gas releases carbon dioxide and other compounds that heat up the atmosphere and contribute to what is known as *global warming*. Because nuclear reactors do not release those compounds into the atmosphere, some are now realizing that nuclear power might decrease the amount of global warming gases that enter the atmosphere.

It is interesting to note that the other sources of energy can also release radioactivity into the environment—and, in some cases, even more radiation than nuclear energy does. For example, because of the way that uranium behaves in the environment, a lot of it can be found in coal. As a result, burning coal can release uranium into the environment; the disposal of coal ash (also called *fly ash*) can also release radioactivity into the environment. A lot of fuel oil also contains small amounts of uranium, so extracting petroleum, refining it to form fuel oil, and then burning it releases radioactivity as well. It turns out that coal and fuel oil power plants, when added together, actually put more radioactivity into the environment than do the entire world's existing nuclear power plants. Natural gas also contains some radioactivity, but not as much as petroleum or coal. So while natural gas plants do release some radioactivity, the amount is less than that released by nuclear reactors. What all of this means is that no form of energy production is perfect—every source presents some potential problem.

One form of energy that seems to have fewer problems than most others is nuclear *fusion* power. Unlike uranium fission (which is how nuclear reactors work), fusion power involves fusing two cores of atoms—or nuclei—in order to form a single, heavier nucleus. For fuel, a fusion reactor uses hydrogen, the lightest nucleus, or uses its slightly heavier cousins, deuterium and tritium. The fusion process actually releases much more energy than nuclear fission, and it produces much less radioactive waste. So many people are excited about the possibility of developing a working hydrogen fusion reactor. (In fact, this type of reactor appears on many science fiction TV shows and movies.) Right now, however, scientists are not having a lot of luck turning fusion power into reality—it is much more difficult than anything else humans have tried to build. Scientists can produce fusion energy, but right now it takes much more energy to create nuclear fusion than the actual energy that fusion gives us in return. In other words, in trying to create nuclear fusion, energy is actually lost instead of gained. While humans can make bombs that use fusion power, they are not yet able to control the reaction for use in a power plant. And even when that point is reached, fusion power will still produce some radioactive waste—just not as much as fission power. So, while fusion power has a lot of promise as a great source of energy for the future, it cannot yet help solve the world's energy problems yet. Still, many scientists around the world are joining together to solve these scientific and technological problems in the hope that fusion will someday be a practical, abundant, and clean source of energy.

THE NUCLEAR FUEL CYCLE

Uranium ore is mined from the ground and sent to a milling facility where the uranium is chemically extracted from the ore. The uranium is then chemically processed to form a uranium-fluoride compound (UF_6) that can be easily turned into reactor fuel. The uranium in UF_6 contains a relatively high concentration of the important U-235 isotope in addition to the U-238 isotope more commonly found in the Earth's crust. While inside the nuclear reactor, much of the U-235 is used up (fissioned) to run the reactor, but at the same time, some of the U-238 is turned into plutonium. When the fuel will no longer support nuclear reactions, it can be reprocessed to remove the remaining useable uranium and the

(continues on page 58)

Fermi's Own Story
by Enrico Fermi

Enrico Fermi was an Italian physicist who won the 1938 Nobel Prize in Physics for his discovery of artificial radioactivity. Fermi was instrumental in designing and constructing the first artificial nuclear reactor.

It is ten years since man first achieved a self-sustaining atomic reaction.

Many people link this event only with the development of the atomic bomb and the subsequent efforts to develop the hydrogen bomb, reference to which has been made in the last few days by the Atomic Energy Commission.

The history of the first self-sustaining nuclear chain reaction, like that of all scientific achievements, begins with man's first philosophical speculations about the nature of the universe. Its ultimate consequences are still unpredictable.

The sequence of discoveries leading to the atomic chain reaction was part of the search of science for a fuller explanation of nature and the world around us. No one had any idea or intent in the beginning of contributing to a major industrial or military development.

A partial list of the main stepping-stones to this development indicates many countries contributed to it.

The story begins in Paris in 1896 when Antoine Henri Becquerel discovered the existence of radioactive elements; that is, elements which spontaneously emit invisible, penetrating rays. Two years later, also in Paris, Pierre and Marie Cure discovered radium, for many years the best known of the radioactive elements.

In Zurich, Switzerland, in 1905, Albert Einstein announced his belief that mass was equivalent to energy. This led to speculation that one could be transformed into the other.

A most important discovery came in 1912 when Ernest Rutherford discovered the minute but heavy nucleus which forms the core of the atom. In ordinary elements this core is stable; in radioactive elements it is unstable.

Shortly after World War I, the same Rutherford achieved for the first time the artificial disintegration of the nucleus at the center of the nitrogen atom.

During the next decade, research progressed steadily, if unspectacularly. Then, in 1932, came a series of three discoveries by scientists working in three different countries which led to the next great advance.

Walter Bothe in Germany, and Frederic Joliot-Curie in Paris prepared the ground work that led James Chadwick of England to the discovery of the neutron. The neutron is an electrically neutral building block of the nuclear structure. The other building block is the positively charged proton.

The next step was taken in Rome in 1934. In experiments in which I was concerned it was shown that these neutrons could disintegrate many atoms, including those of uranium. This discovery was to be directly applied in the first atomic chain reaction eight years later.

The Discovery of Fission

The final stepping-stone was put in place in Berlin when Otto Hahn, working with Fritz Strassman, discovered fission or splitting of the uranium atom. When Hahn achieved fission, it occurred to many scientists that this fact opened the possibility of a form of nuclear (atomic) energy.

The year was 1939. A world war was about to start. The new possibilities appeared likely to be important, not only for peace but also for war.

A group of physicists in the United States (including Leo Szilard, Walter Zinn, now director of Argonne National Laboratory, Herbert Anderson, and myself) agreed privately to delay further publications of findings in this field.

We were afraid these findings might help the Nazis. Our action, of course, represented a break with scientific tradition and was not taken lightly. Subsequently, when the government became interested in the atom bomb project, secrecy became compulsory.

(continues)

(continued)

Here it may be well to define what is meant by the "chain reaction" which was to constitute our next objective in the search for a method of utilizing atomic energy.

An atomic chain reaction may be compared to the burning of a rubbish pile from spontaneous combustion. In such a fire, minute parts of the pile start to burn and in turn ignite other tiny fragments. When sufficient numbers of these fractional parts are heated to the kindling points, the entire heap bursts into flames.

A similar process takes place in an atomic pile such as was constructed under the West Stands of Stagg Field at The University of Chicago in 1942.

The pile itself was constructed of uranium, a material that is embedded in a matrix of graphite. With sufficient uranium in the pile, the few neutrons emitted in a single fission that may accidentally occur strike neighboring atoms, which in turn undergo fission and produce more neutrons.

These bombard other atoms and so on at an increasing rate until the atomic "fire" is going full blast.

The atomic pile is controlled and prevented from burning itself to complete destruction by cadmium rods which absorb neutrons and stop the bombardment process. The same effect might be achieved by running a pipe of cold water through a rubbish heap; by keeping the temperature low the pipe would prevent the spontaneous burning.

The first atomic chain reaction experiment was designed to proceed at a slow rate. In this sense it differed from the atomic bomb, which was designed to proceed at as fast a rate as was possible. Otherwise, the basic process is similar to that of the atomic bomb.

The atomic chain reaction was the result of hard work by many hands and many heads. Arthur H. Compton, Walter Zinn, Herbert Anderson, Leo Szilard, Eugene Wigner and many others worked directly on the problems at The University of Chicago. Very many experiments and calculations had to be performed. Finally a plan was decided upon.

Thirty "piles" of less than the size necessary to establish a chain reaction were built and tested. Then the plans were made for the final test of a full-sized pile.

The scene of this test at The University of Chicago would have been confusing to an outsider—if he could have eluded the security guards and gained admittance.

He would have seen only what appeared to be a crude pile of black bricks and wooden timbers. All but one side of the pile was obscured by a balloon cloth envelope.

As the pile grew toward its final shape during the days of preparation, the measurement performed many times a day indicated everything was going, if anything, a little bit better than predicted by calculations.

The Gathering on the Balcony

Finally, the day came when we were ready to run the experiment. We gathered on a balcony about 10 feet above the floor of the large room in which the structure had been erected.

Beneath us was a young scientist, George Weil, whose duty it was to handle the last control rod that was holding the reaction in check.

Every precaution had been taken against an accident. There were three sets of control rods in the pile. One set was automatic. Another consisted of a heavily weighted emergency safety held by a rope. Walter Zinn was holding the rope, ready to release it at the least sign of trouble.

The last rod left in the pile, which acted as starter, accelerator and brake for the reaction, was the one handled by Weil.

Since the experiment had never been tried before, a "liquid control squad" stood ready to flood the pile with cadmium salt solution in case the control rods failed. Before we began, we rehearsed the safety precautions carefully.

Finally, it was time to remove the control rods. Slowly, Weil started to withdraw the main control rod. On the balcony, we watched the indicators which measured the neutron count and told us how rapidly the disintegration of the uranium atoms under their neutron bombardment was proceeding.

(continues)

(continued)

At 11:35 A.M., the counters were clicking rapidly. Then, with a loud clap, the automatic control rods slammed home. The safety point had been set too low.

It seemed a good time to eat lunch.

During lunch everyone was thinking about the experiment but nobody talked much about it.

At 2:30, Weil pulled out the control rod in a series of measured adjustments.

Shortly after, the intensity shown by the indicators began to rise at a slow but ever-increasing rate. At this moment we knew that the self-sustaining reaction was under way.

The event was not spectacular, no fuses burned, no lights flashed. But to us it meant that release of atomic energy on a large scale would be only a matter of time.

The further development of atomic energy during the next three years of the war was, of course, focused on the main objective of producing an effective weapon.

At the same time we all hoped that with the end of the war emphasis would be shifted decidedly from the weapon to the peaceful aspects of atomic energy.

We hoped that perhaps the building of power plants, production of radioactive elements for science and medicine would become the paramount objectives.

Unfortunately, the end of the war did not bring brotherly love among nations. The fabrication of weapons still is and must be the primary concern of the Atomic Energy Commission.

Secrecy that we thought was an unwelcome necessity of the war still appears to be an unwelcome necessity. The peaceful objectives must come second, although very considerable progress has been made also along those lines.

The problems posed by this world situation are not for the scientist alone but for all people to resolve. Perhaps a time will come when all scientific and technical progress will be hailed for the advantages that it may bring to man, and never feared on account of its destructive possibilities.

Reprinted in *The First Reactor*, Published December, 1982, by the U.S Department of Energy.

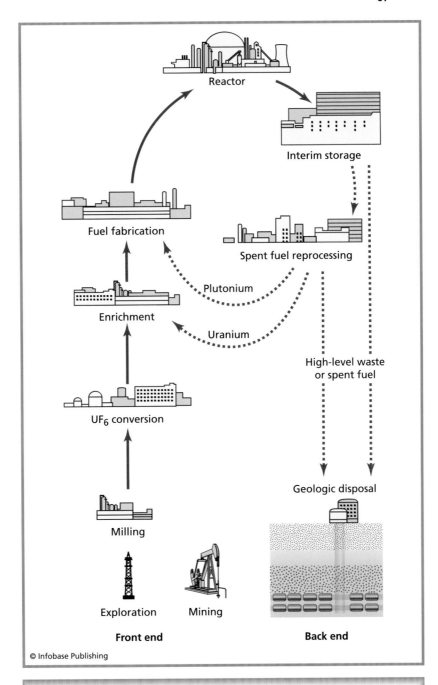

Reactor

Interim storage

Fuel fabrication

Spent fuel reprocessing

Plutonium

Enrichment

Uranium

High-level waste
or spent fuel

UF₆ conversion

Geologic disposal

Milling

Exploration   Mining

Front end   **Back end**

© Infobase Publishing

Figure 4.3   The nuclear fuel cycle shows the steps of how nuclear fuel is obtained, expended, and then reprocessed or stored as waste.

(continued from page 51)

plutonium. These can then be recycled into new reactor fuel. Or, because the plutonium can also be used to make nuclear weapons, the spent reactor fuel can be buried underground so it cannot be used to make weapons.

The Dark Side
of Radiation:
Nuclear Weapons
and Terrorism

October 9, 2006, 10:30 A.M.: An alert person would have noticed that the seismograph was trembling a little, showing that the ground underneath Japan had just been shaken. The size of the tremor suggested a small earthquake, a little over magnitude 4. This was not surprising since Japan is one of the most seismically active places on Earth. But this one was different; it didn't look exactly like a typical earthquake. As time went on, the scientists found out why. In the next few days, airplanes flying over the Sea of Japan and the Yellow Sea, as well as south of the Korean Demilitarized Zone, detected radioactive gases, most likely nuclides of krypton and xenon—the hallmarks of nuclear fission, the splitting of cores of atoms to release large amounts of energy. These gases, plus the "earthquake," confirmed that North Korea had become the most recent member of the most exclusive club on Earth—the group of nations that possess nuclear weapons. With North Korea, this club now numbers nine and also includes the United States, Russia, Great Britain, France, China, Israel, India, and Pakistan. (South Africa had developed nuclear weapons, but dismantled them and destroyed its nuclear weapons program in the 1980s.) Nuclear weapons also had been based in several nations that were once part of the Soviet Union, but all of them returned their weapons to Russia when the Soviet Union dissolved in the early 1990s.

North Korea had tested a very small nuclear device. Those outside the country still are not really sure how large the explosion was supposed to be, but the available information suggests that it may have been one of the smallest nuclear explosions ever recorded. For this reason, many scientists wondered if there had been some problems, or even wondered if it was a real nuclear weapon. Eventually, people agreed that it was, but that it had probably not exploded as planned.

Today there is a great deal of concern about nuclear weapons. With North Korea now testing nuclear weapons, the world is now also worried that Iran might develop them. Not long ago, it seemed that India and Pakistan might even launch nuclear strikes against each other. In the 1950s and 1960s, people worried that the Soviet Union and the United States would have a nuclear war that would destroy both of these nations and many other countries as well. Why are people so afraid of nuclear weapons, and why are nations so afraid that their enemies will develop them? This chapter will tackle these questions, and will also discuss other ways that nuclear and radioactive materials might be used to hurt people.

HOW NUCLEAR WEAPONS WORK

As described in Chapter 4, the cores of uranium atoms—their nuclei—release a lot of energy when they split apart, or fission. In a nuclear reactor, that energy is released slowly and in a controlled manner. A **nuclear weapon** makes the nuclei split apart more rapidly and in an uncontrolled fashion. It is like the difference between burning a log in the fireplace and blowing up a stick of dynamite. Both release similar amounts of total energy, but the fact that the wood burns so slowly (and that the dynamite burns so rapidly) makes all the difference between a room that becomes warm and one that blows up.

To understand how nuclear weapons are made, it is important to learn what is meant by a **critical mass** of uranium or plutonium. And to understand that, it is important to learn a little more about how nuclear fission works.

If a uranium or plutonium nucleus gets hit with a neutron, it often splits into two pieces. In addition, when a nucleus splits (or fissions), it releases two or three neutrons. *Nuclear criticality* occurs when one of these neutrons goes on to fission another nucleus. When a nuclear reaction becomes "critical," it is simply releasing energy at a steady, constant rate, which is what happens in a nuclear reactor. But if *two* neutrons from each fission end up causing another fission, then there is an increase in the rate of energy that is released: It doubles with every set of fissions. And, because the fissions happen so rapidly, this leads to an explosive release of energy.

In other words, a critical mass is the amount of uranium or plutonium that is needed to keep a nuclear chain reaction going. But it needs to be formed in the right shape, as well. In a flat sheet of uranium, the only way that a neutron can cause additional fission is for that neutron to be emitted in exactly the right direction so it strikes another uranium or plutonium atom. If the neutron is emitted in any other direction than directly within the sheet, it will simply escape and be lost. So, in addition to having the right amount of material, that material has to be in the right shape: This is called the *critical geometry.*

A nuclear weapon starts off with a critical mass of uranium or plutonium that is not yet in a critical geometry. Explosives are used to change the shape of the uranium or plutonium, so that it reaches critical geometry. At that point, the nuclear chain reaction can take place, and the weapon explodes.

THE EFFECTS OF NUCLEAR WEAPONS

On August 6, 1945, the Japanese city of Hiroshima was almost completely destroyed by a single bomb dropped by a single airplane. More than 100,000 people died, and many more were injured. Three days later, another Japanese city, Nagasaki, was destroyed by a second nuclear weapon—again, a single bomb dropped by a single airplane. On August 15, the Japanese emperor announced Japan's surrender,

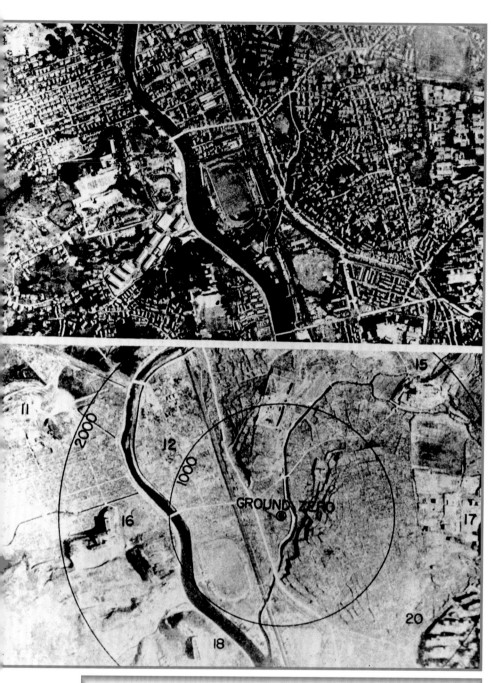

Figure 5.1 Nagasaki was a bustling city before the atomic bomb was dropped (*top*). The circles on the barren land following the explosion (*bottom*) indicate distance in thousands of feet from ground zero.

ending World War II. The two nuclear weapons were so destructive that the Japanese simply could not justify continuing to fight.

Over the next few decades, several other nations developed their own nuclear weapons—France and Great Britain were allies of the United States, while the Soviet Union and China were communist opponents. All of the nuclear powers tested their weapons, first in the open atmosphere and later in underground tunnels. These tests helped to demonstrate the incredible destructive power of nuclear weapons, and made everyone aware of how dangerous they could be. And, as weapons designers became better and better at their jobs, the nuclear weapons became even more destructive, including hydrogen (thermonuclear) bombs, which use the same nuclear fusion reaction that powers the Sun. Thermonuclear weapons are at least 10 times as destructive as "ordinary" nuclear bombs. In fact, they are the most destructive explosives on the planet.

When a nuclear weapon explodes, it gives off radiation, heat, and a blast wave. The radiation from an explosion can injure people, as we saw in Chapter 3. The heat can start fires, maybe as much as a few miles away from the blast, and burn and destroy everything within that distance. The blast wave will knock buildings down, also out to a distance of a few miles. In this way, a single weapon can kill a city in a moment, and this is why humanity spent nearly a half century worrying about a large-scale nuclear war.

RADIOLOGICAL TERRORISM

In the last few years, the United States and many European nations have grown worried that terrorists might try to attack using nuclear or radiological weapons.

In general, a radiological weapon is one in which terrorists would simply add radioactive materials to a "normal" bomb—this weapon is called a **radiological dispersal device** (RDD), also known as a **dirty bomb**. When it explodes, it scatters the radioactive materials over a large area. The purpose is to frighten people and cause city officials to shut down parts of the city because of the radioactive contamination. The law requires that places with radioactive contamination must be cleaned up before people can return to them.

If a dirty bomb were set off in Manhattan, for example, the explosion itself might first kill people and harm buildings and also spread radioactivity around a large area. Everyone in the area would be contaminated, and they might need to be cleaned up before being allowed to go home. After that, the contaminated section of the city would have to be cleaned up before it could be used again. Until that time, the stores, restaurants, and businesses in that area would have to be closed. In addition, it may take a long time—many months, or even years—to clean everything up to where it would be safe enough for people to return. Parts of Manhattan might be closed for months, or years. This would likely cost billions of dollars or more in **cleanup** efforts and lost business.

But what most people do not know is that the radiation and radioactivity from a dirty bomb attack are not likely to hurt anyone. This is because no one can carry highly radioactive materials for long without getting very sick themselves, and the most powerful radioactive sources are hard to conceal and transport: Such attackers are likely to become too ill or be captured before carrying out their plans. If they were somehow to be successful, the radioactivity in a dirty bomb would most likely come from a weaker source of radiation. Even those people caught in the area when the bomb goes off are not likely to be exposed to enough radiation to cause them to get sick. This is something important to remember—and important enough to say again. Very few people, even those who are in the area of a dirty bomb attack, are likely to be exposed to enough radiation to make them sick. In fact, it is entirely possible that nobody will develop radiation sickness from a dirty bomb attack. Too little radiation would probably be spread out over too large an area to have much effect. It is possible that some people might develop cancer 20 years or more after the attack, but it is not possible to estimate how many for the reasons discussed in Chapter 3.

So, radiological terrorism is not much different than any other form of terrorism—the explosion from a dirty bomb attack might hurt no more people than any other explosion would. After the explosion, the government might be forced to spend a lot of money in cleaning up (decontaminating) the area that was attacked. But most scientists do not expect very many health problems as a result of a radiological terrorist attack, even though it is likely to frighten a lot of people and to cost a lot of money for the cleanup.

STAYING SAFE AFTER AN ATTACK

Whether an attack is nuclear or radiological, there are some things that people can do to stay safe as long as they are far enough away from the explosion itself. The best protection is to go inside a building and shut all of the doors and windows to shield against radioactivity that has been released into the air. For those who cannot get inside, cars are the next best shelter. If the attack takes place on a hot day, it is a good idea to turn on the air conditioning, as long as it is set to recirculate the air inside the car.

Anyone outside at the time of an attack could be contaminated by radioactivity. Once they get inside, they should change their clothes and take a shower to wash the contamination off of their skin and out of their hair. Unless a person is very close to the explosion, he or she will have a pretty low radiation dose; by changing clothes and taking a shower, the radiation dose will be even lower. One other thing people should do is to stay inside and turn on the radio or television to find out what is happening and what the risks are. Being inside is safer than being outside, and it should not take the local authorities very long to find out where the contamination is and to be able to give good advice.

About the worst thing that anyone can do is to try to drive away in their car after a dirty bomb attack. Being in a car on the road is likely to be about the most dangerous place of all. In fact, driving is even more dangerous than getting a small dose of radiation. A road full of motorists can make it more difficult for the firefighters and ambulances to reach the scene, and more difficult for the ambulances to take injured people to the hospitals. This is doubly bad—trying to drive away makes things more dangerous for both the drivers and for those trying to help. Of course, those who are close to the site of the attack should try to get away, but it is probably safer to walk away than to drive, for those who are able to do so. Also, radioactivity will be carried by the wind. Those walking away from the scene of a blast should first determine which way the wind is blowing from, and then walk *across* the wind. In other words, if the wind is blowing from north to south, they should walk to the east or the west.

One last thing: Those who are close to an explosion should avoid eating or drinking anything until they are away from the contamination area and get cleaned up. Otherwise, they might accidentally eat radioactivity, which could deliver a higher dose of radiation. If they must have to eat something, they should try to clean the food off first, and try to move as far as possible from the

Table 5.1: Nuclear Proliferation Timeline	
1945	First U.S. nuclear weapons test; United States explodes first nuclear weapons in Japan
1949	USSR conducts first nuclear test
1952	United Kingdom conducts first nuclear test; U.S. tests first thermonuclear device
1953	USSR tests first thermonuclear device
1960	France conducts first nuclear test
1963	Atmospheric test ban treaty bans "open air" nuclear weapons testing for signatories
1964	China tests first nuclear device
1967	China tests first thermonuclear device
1968	France tests first thermonuclear device
1974	India tests first nuclear device
1979	"Vela Incident"—possible nuclear test by South Africa or Israel in the South Atlantic
1990s	A.Q. Khan (Pakistan) begins selling nuclear weapons technology to other nations
1996	Osama bin Laden announces determination to obtain nuclear weapons
1998	Pakistan tests first nuclear device
2006	North Korea tests first nuclear device

Figure 5.2 The Atomic Dome, as it came to be known, was the closest building to ground zero to survive the atomic bomb. It has been preserved in the same state as it was following the bombing as part of the Peace Memorial Park, while the rest of Hiroshima was rebuilt around it.

site of the attack to reduce their exposure to radioactivity as much as possible.

Finally, people need to remember that a radiological or nuclear attack may be dangerous, and it will certainly be frightening. But unless they are close enough to be directly involved in the attack—that would be within about 5 to 10 miles (8-16 km) of a nuclear attack or within sight or hearing of a dirty bomb attack—they are not likely to be at risk.

6

Radiation in the Environment

There are many concerns about the release of radioactivity into the environment. Some nuclear accidents have released radioactivity—sometimes a great deal of it. Nuclear reactors produce radioactive waste that must be disposed of, usually by burying it in a landfill. Some nations, including the United States, use depleted uranium—a reduced-radioactivity version of uranium metal—for military and defense applications, such as durable armor plating or tank-penetrating artillery. When used in artillery, the depleted uranium winds up on the ground where it might spread. Radioactive fallout from nuclear weapons testing has also entered the environment, and a radiological or nuclear attack would release even more radioactivity into the environment. All of this radioactivity might travel through the environment to reach other organisms, including humans. This chapter will describe how radioactivity can get into the environment and, once there, how it can spread to humans and other organisms: These routes are called **exposure pathways**. It will also discuss radioactive waste, how it is stored, and what happens when other forms of radioactivity, such as nuclear weapons fallout and radioactivity from accidents, enter the environment.

EXPOSURE PATHWAYS

Radioactivity released into the environment enters the air, the soil, or the water. From there, it can follow any number of pathways to reach people: for example, through the air that people breathe. It can also settle onto the ground, and make its way into plants. From there, it can be ingested by both animals and people. When people eat meat or drink milk contaminated by this radiation, they would also be exposed to radioactivity.

Following are some of the more well-known exposure pathways. All of these paths and more can be taken, for example, from radioactivity that has been emitted into the air from a nuclear reactor plant:

Air–inhalation
Air–ground–plants–ingestion
Air–ground–plants–cows–meat–ingestion
Air–ground–plants–cows–milk–ingestion
Air–ground–groundwater–ingestion
Air–ground–groundwater–plants–ingestion
Air–surface water–fish–ingestion
Air–surface water–ground water–plants–ingestion

There are many exposure pathways, and the ones listed here are only a few. In general, the more links in an exposure pathway, the more the radioactivity is diluted, or weakened, and the lower the exposure to people at the end of the pathway.

RADIOACTIVE WASTE

The use of radioactive materials, including in nuclear power plants, always produces radioactive waste. Like any other sort of waste, radioactive waste takes many forms. Hospitals and universities create a lot of radioactive waste, mostly in objects like paper towels, test tubes, and the plastic gloves that people wear to keep their hands from being **contaminated** with radioactivity. Other kinds of radioactive waste generated at hospitals and universities include syringes, laboratory glassware, surgical masks, and other equipment

Exposure Path

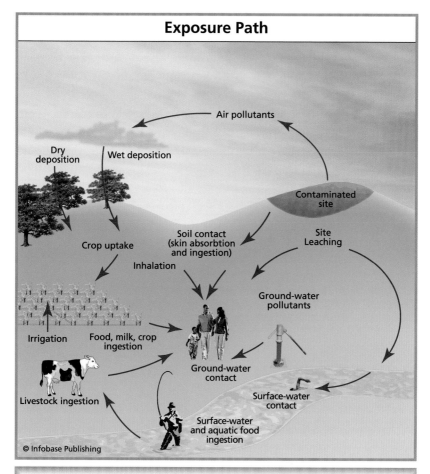

Air pollutants

Dry deposition

Wet deposition

Contaminated site

Crop uptake

Soil contact (skin absorbtion and ingestion)

Site Leaching

Inhalation

Ground-water pollutants

Irrigation

Food, milk, crop ingestion

Livestock ingestion

Ground-water contact

Surface-water contact

Surface-water and aquatic food ingestion

© Infobase Publishing

Figure 6.1 Radioactivity released into the environment can reach people through a number of exposure pathways.

that is used in research or in medical treatment. The nuclear power industry produces several different kinds of radioactive waste. **High-level radioactive waste** includes any used nuclear reactor fuel and any of the waste that is produced when it is recycled. All other forms of radioactive waste are called **low-level radioactive waste**. However, even some forms of low-level radioactive waste can be very radioactive, so there are different categories here too— Class A, Class B, and Class C. There is also an extra category (the most dangerous) called "Greater than Class C." This is all pretty confusing, and hard to keep track of. To simplify things a little bit, this section will discuss the most dangerous waste (called "high level"). Everything else will be called "low-level waste." For the most part, low-level radioactive waste is classified as either Class A or B, and it is no more dangerous than any other kind of waste. For example, consider what happens when someone decides to throw away a lot of cleaning products from underneath the kitchen counter or the basement. Many of these products are poisons that are dangerous to drink or spill on the skin. Once they wind up in the trash, they are taken to a landfill where they are dumped in with napkins, eggshells, banana peels, and other garbage. These poisons are as dangerous—in many cases more dangerous—as low-level radioactive waste. When a house gets a new roof, the old roof is taken to a landfill for disposal—along with other construction waste from all the other buildings that are being built, renovated, or torn down. Because roofs contain solvents and other compounds, this waste is about as dangerous, and in some cases more dangerous, than most low-level radioactive waste. In other words, most low-level radioactive waste can be disposed of in landfills as many other products are, so long as the landfills are well designed to handle it. Most low-level radioactive waste is packed into 55-gallon drums, which are then taken to a radioactive waste landfill. The landfill is lined with clay, which helps to keep water out of the landfill and radioactive liquids away from the **groundwater**. Many landfills have this design, including those that are used for hazardous chemical wastes, construction waste, and others. High-level radioactive waste can be far more dangerous, so it has to be treated much more carefully. High-level radioactive waste is often sealed in large containers made of steel and concrete, which are designed to reduce radiation levels as well as to seal in the radioactivity. At the moment, these containers are being stored at the individual nuclear power plants, because there is no location in the United States where they can be safely stored for the thousands of years needed for their radioactivity to decay. However, the long-term plan is for the United States to open a high-level radioactive waste disposal site specially constructed for the most dangerous wastes. This site is being built under a mountain in the Nevada desert, and it is designed to keep the waste safe, secure, and away from people for thousands of years. At the moment, there is a lot of controversy about the safety of this

High-level Radioactive Waste Container

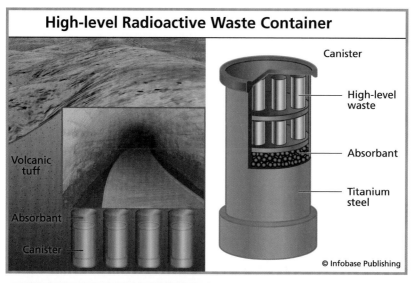

Canister

High-level waste

Absorbant

Titanium steel

Volcanic tuff

Absorbant

Canister

© Infobase Publishing

Figure 6.2 Waste containers for high-level radioactive waste (*top*) are made to reduce the radiation levels by sealing in radioactive material. Low-level waste containers are unloaded and staged before disposal at the Area 5 Waste Management Site on the Nevada Test Site.

site, and many people are not sure if this is the best way to dispose of such dangerous materials. Even though there are some concerns about this location, proponents argue that the natural geology of the location is well known enough to ensure that it will be a safe place to dispose of this high-level radioactive waste.

NUCLEAR WEAPONS TESTING AND RADIOLOGICAL ACCIDENTS

Chapter 4 discussed some nuclear reactor accidents in terms of what took place within the nuclear reactor, but not about what the effects were on the environment. There have been many other incidents during which radioactivity was released into the environment. These include the atmospheric nuclear weapons testing mentioned briefly in Chapter 6, the use of depleted uranium in warfare, and some accidents that took place in the former Soviet Union.

Atmospheric Nuclear Weapons Testing

Every split—or fission—of a single atomic nucleus produces two nuclei, both of which are radioactive. A nuclear explosion creates a lot of radioactivity because the energy released is the result of the fission of a great many atoms. Between 1945 and 1963, a number of nations tested nuclear weapons in the atmosphere or underwater in the ocean. A total of 543 nuclear tests were conducted in the atmosphere by nations including the United States (219), the Soviet Union (219), France (50), Great Britain (33), and China (22), with a total nuclear yield of 440 megatons, of which 189 megatons came from nuclear fission and the remainder from nuclear fusion. (Nuclear fission produces radioactive fission fragments, while thermonuclear fusion does not. For this reason, a fusion reaction, although more powerful than a fission reaction, is considered a "clean" explosion.) A megaton is equivalent to the blast created by a million tons (2,000,000 pounds) of TNT. A single megaton is an explosive amount of material, able to destroy 80 square miles in a single blast.

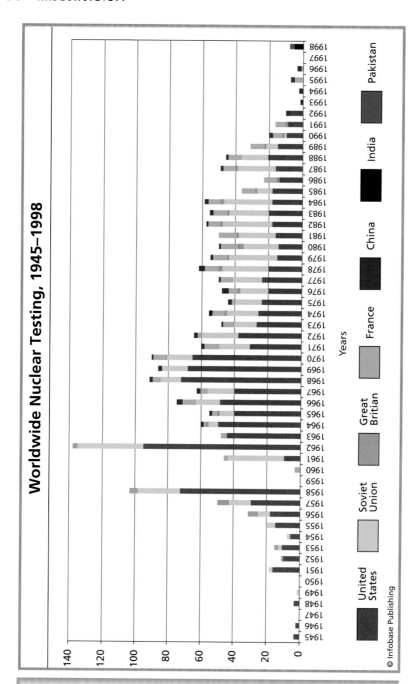

Figure 6.3 Atmospheric nuclear weapons testing in different countries between 1945 and 1998 was highest in 1962.

But this does not fully convey the impact of past nuclear tests on the environment. These explosions deposited over 500 million curies of long-lived radioactivity into the environment. (Remember how radioactivity decays over time; a curie is the amount of material that undergoes 37,000,000,000 radioactivity events, such as fissions or decays, per second.) Some types of radioactive atoms, or nuclides, decay rapidly—they are said to be short lived. After a nuclear explosion, the short-lived nuclides will decay away and be gone within a year or so. But the long-lived nuclides from the same explosion will take much longer to decay away, maybe centuries or millennia. This radioactivity spread all over the world, although most of it remained in the Northern Hemisphere where most of the nuclear test sites were located. Another 1,876 tests were conducted in tunnels deep underground, with a total yield of 90 megatons.

Of the 543 "atmospheric" nuclear weapons tests, 46 of them were conducted on a barge on the water (or underwater) and 17 were conducted in the high atmosphere or in outer space. The other 480 were exploded in the open air, either on the surface or on a tower above the ground. The radioactivity from these tests ended up in the atmosphere, in surface waters (oceans, lakes, rivers, and streams), and settled out onto the ground. From there, some of the radioactivity made it into the groundwater, into plants, into the food chain, and into humans. With the signing of the 1963 Nuclear Test-Ban Treaty, all nuclear testing had to be conducted deep underground to reduce the amount of radiation entering the environment. However, nuclear weapons are so powerful that even some underground tests "vented" radioactivity into the environment, though not nearly as much as the atmospheric tests.

Nuclear Reactor Accidents

As mentioned in Chapter 4, several accidents at nuclear reactor plants have taken place around the world. Some of these accidents released radioactivity into the environment, although with only a few exceptions, they did not seriously affect residents in the area. One well-known accident involved the Three Mile Island nuclear reactor in Pennsylvania. Although the Three Mile Island accident received a great deal of press coverage, it did not have a

Figure 6.4 Abandoned apartment buildings in Pripyat, two miles from the site of Chernobyl's accident. Pripyat, where Chernobyl workers once lived, remains a ghost town.

significant effect on the environment. In fact, the radiation dose received by those living near the nuclear power plant was low enough that, in 2001 and 2002, U.S. Federal courts decided that there was no reason to believe that anyone had been harmed by the accident.

The most serious accident was at the Chernobyl nuclear power plant in what is now the Ukraine near the city of Kiev. In addition to its immediate effects, the Chernobyl accident released about 180 million curies of long-lived radioactivity to the environment. That is more than one-third of the total amount of radioactivity released by all of the atmospheric nuclear weapons testing combined. This radioactivity was distributed throughout the Northern Hemisphere, with the highest concentrations in Europe, particularly in the area around Chernobyl.

Following the accident, the Soviet Union forced the evacuation of over 300,000 people from the area around Chernobyl. They then restricted access to the area surrounding the nuclear power plant—it remains restricted more than 20 years later.

Many plants and animals died from high radiation exposure in the first months following the accident. But what is interesting is that, after a decade, the restricted area around Chernobyl became among the richest ecologies in Europe, with growing numbers of moose, deer, bears, wild boar, and other animals. From this perspective, building roads, farms, and houses had a greater impact on the environment due to habitat loss than the radioactivity from the Chernobyl accident. This is not to say that Chernobyl caused no harm—it did cause many human deaths and the high radiation levels killed many plants and animals, and some of the returning animals have shown evidence of genetic abnormalities. So Chernobyl was harmful, but scientific evidence suggests it was neither *as* harmful nor *as* long-lasting as most people might think.

What Is Depleted Uranium?

Natural uranium has two primary isotopes, U-235 and U-238. In nature, 99.2% of all uranium atoms are the isotope U-238, which does not easily fission, or split up into nuclear fragments. U-235 atoms comprise virtually all of the rest (0.72%), and U-235 fissions very easily. However, the low concentration of U-235 in natural uranium makes it nearly impossible to sustain a fission chain reaction. To make nuclear reactor fuel, or to make a nuclear weapon, it is necessary to increase, or "enrich," the amount of U-235. This process is called uranium enrichment.

During the enrichment process, some patches of the incoming raw uranium material end up with more U-235 than natural uranium, which is called "enriched uranium." The rest of the uranium (called the "tails") has less U-235 than does natural uranium; this is called "depleted uranium

(continues)

(continued)

(DU)." In effect, uranium enrichment involves concentrating the U-235 atoms into a region of the original mixture of the uranium material and enriching it in that part, with the rest becoming depleted U-235.

Uses for Depleted Uranium

DU is useless for nuclear reactors because it is difficult to fission, and what fission there is does not release very much energy. However, a lot of DU is made in the process of making fuel for nuclear reactors and nuclear weapons. Any DU that is not used must be treated as waste. Because disposing of so much waste is very expensive, governments have found several uses for DU.

Uranium is a metal—and a heavy one at that. But while DU material is very heavy, it is not very radioactive at all. Because of this, DU can be used to make radiation shields—in fact, DU is more effective at blocking radiation than lead and is very useful for shielding against intense radioactive sources. It is also sometimes used for particle accelerators in scientific research, for industry, or for medical treatment.

DU is also used in airplanes for making heavy counterweights that help operate the plane's "control surfaces." These surfaces enable the airplane to change its altitude and heading. In military tanks, DU makes a very good armor to help protect tank crews from enemy fire. Ironically, the only thing that is usually able to penetrate DU armor is DU ammunition. As a result, the United States and a few other nations use DU ammunition to shoot at tanks.

NUCLEAR FUEL AND WEAPONS PRODUCTION CLEANUP

The last chapter discussed nuclear weapons and the nations that have made them. There is a great deal of work that goes into making nuclear weapons, and much of this work involves radio-activity. Many nuclear weapons facilities have released radioactivity into the environment in the United States, the former Soviet Union, and Great Britain, and many of these releases have affected the environment.

In some cases, the environmental contamination was the result of well-intended activities that later turned out to be ill-advised. For example, pollutants in water are removed by contact with clay minerals in soils; so, many facilities would purify radioactively contaminated water by releasing it into the soil. The water would emerge much cleaner, but the soils were left with high levels of contamination. Now, decades later, a lot of money is being spent to clean up this contamination and to restore the environment to how it had been before the nuclear weapons plants began operation. In the United States, many hundreds of billions of dollars have been spent at facilities such as Rocky Flats (in Colorado), Hanford (Washington), Fernald (Ohio), and elsewhere. The U.S. nuclear facilities are well known, but there were also regular releases of radioactivity from many of the Soviet-era nuclear weapons facilities in Russia and the former Soviet states. In fact, many of these facilities were contaminated far more seriously than even the most highly contaminated sites in the United States and elsewhere. In some cases, entire lakes or rivers became dangerously radioactive, and radioactive dust was blown by winds across large areas. Cleaning up these sites may take decades, if it can even be done. And some of these areas will remain dangerously radioactive for decades to come.

Cleaning up Contaminated Sites

A site that has been contaminated with radioactive material must be cleaned up. This is a little more complicated than cleaning up someone's house—it can cost tens of billions of dollars and take years, even decades, of work. It can also take a long time to clean up contaminated water—both surface water (such as rivers, lakes, and streams) and groundwater. Each of these situations has its own problems and its own solutions.

For water that has been contaminated, engineers can build a water treatment plant similar to those that are used to purify drinking water or to treat water from the sewers. The water is passed through filters to remove any particles and is also passed through other purification equipment to remove other contaminants. Sometimes, when the water is located underground, it is necessary to drill wells down to it and pump it out so it can be treated.

Contaminated soil can simply be dug up and then moved to a radioactive waste site where it is buried with other radioactive waste. It can also be washed to remove the radioactive contamination. Yet another form of cleanup (also called **remediation**) is to turn the contaminated soil into glass, a process called *vitrification*. In some cases, the contaminated soil is dug up and passed through a vitrification facility that turns the soil into glass pellets (*vitrification* comes from *vitro*, the Latin word for glass.) The pellets can then be shipped out for disposal.

Another option is to ship the waste to the Nevada Test Site, the area where the United States used to conduct nuclear weapons tests. These tests left behind craters that are now used for radioactive waste disposal.

7

The Bright Side of Radiation: In the Hospital, Laboratory, Supermarket, and Home

During a typical day, many people start by waking up in the morning, getting out of bed, and brushing their teeth. After breakfast, they may take a bus to school and spend the day in class reading, writing, and working on the computer. They then return home, have a snack and work on homework, and eat dinner. Later on, they might watch TV and then go to bed. Other days might be different, maybe taken up with traveling on vacation, or playing soccer, or (hopefully not!) paying a visit to the doctor's office or the hospital. The question here is, during their day, how often do they encounter manmade radiation?

Most companies that manufacture medical or dental products (including many toothpaste manufacturers) do their initial research using radioactivity. They do not include radioactivity as an ingredient in the toothpaste they sell, but they probably use it during laboratory testing on animals. For example, it may have been added to molecules in the toothpaste to see if any of them are absorbed into the bloodstream through the lining of the mouth. In addition, once or twice a year, a dentist will probably take X-rays—a form of radiation—of their patients' teeth.

And there is a good chance that there is some natural radioactivity in the porcelain in most sinks and toilet bowls (probably potassium-40) and maybe even some uranium and its decay byproducts that are contained in the clays that make up the porcelain. So, before most people even finish dressing, they have probably come across radiation, radioactivity, or products where it was used during the production process at least a few times. Although clothing does not contain radioactivity, clothes made of natural fibers (cotton or wool, for example) may have been subject to radioactivity at some point during the research that was done to help make these products better.

Breakfast is likely the next point where most people will encounter the results of radiation or radioactivity use—a lot of agricultural research uses radioactivity to help grow better crops. For example, scientists have "sequenced," or decoded, the genomes— the full blueprint of genetic instructions—of quite a few crops. The DNA molecules that make up a crop's genome contain a kind of "alphabet" of four letters (A, T, C, and G). The sequence of letters in the crop genome (for example, AACTTG . . .) provides instructions for producing proteins that enable it to grow from a tiny seed into nourishing food. To determine the crop's genetic code, laboratory scientists often attach radioactive substances such as phosphorus-32 to the DNA molecules. These radioactive "labels" help them detect and track the different letters in the crop's genetic sequence.

Some plants have been genetically engineered to make them resistant to insects or disease, to make them produce more grain or fruit, to help them survive extreme weather, and so forth. Virtually all of the research that went into developing better plants was done in a laboratory that used radioactivity for this work—to help to identify genes, to sequence them, to learn what proteins they help to form, and so forth. There is a good chance that radioactivity played a part in the development of the grains in cereal or bread, and the orange or grapefruit trees that the juice came from.

In addition to agricultural research, radiation and radioactivity cross most breakfast eaters' paths in another way that is called "process control." For example, factory gauges use radioactivity to make sure that the cardboard used to make cereal boxes is precisely the right thickness—not too thick and not too thin. Radiation may have been used to help dry the ink used in printing the cereal box and milk container. Radiation may have also been used to help ensure that the orange juice container was completely full before it was sent to the store.

Radiation is also used to destroy harmful bacteria and other microbes in food. This is similar to pasteurizing milk, in which heating up the milk kills microbes. In food irradiation, X-rays can kill salmonella bacteria in meat and poultry. Once the X-rays strike the food, they transfer their energy into killing the microbes; then they disappear, just as light disappears when a black piece of paper absorbs it, so no radiation remains. This is similar to what happens at the dentist—teeth do not become radioactive after being struck with X-rays. Their energy goes into making patterns in the film that show pictures of the teeth. But can X-rays create dangerous chemical compounds in food? Scientists have thoroughly tested the food for such **radiolytic** compounds, but have not found any evidence for toxic byproducts.

Through the rest of their day, people will encounter even more things that were developed or manufactured with the help of radiation. Brakes, for example, are X-rayed to make sure that they will do their job of safely stopping school buses, cars, or airplanes. The nuts and bolts that hold all of these vehicles together are also checked with radiation, and other forms of radiation are used to make sure that these parts are made of exactly the right mixture of metals. And the thickness of the materials that make up the bus, car, or airplane is gauged using radiation and radioactive materials. For electrical products used at home (lights, televisions, radios, and computers, among others), there is a chance that some of the electrical power came from a nuclear reactor. Twenty percent of U.S. electricity comes from nuclear power. In short, virtually every aspect of life puts people into contact with something radioactive or something made with the help of radiation or radioactivity. This chapter will further discuss how radiation touches human lives—the bright side of radiation—starting with how radiation is used in medicine.

RADIATION IN MEDICINE

Radiation is indispensable in medicine. Dental X-rays, three-dimensional X-ray scans of the lungs, brain imaging with radioactive particles, radiation therapy for cancer—all of these expose the patient to radiation, and all are necessary to try to preserve (or to regain) human health. The following section will describe how they work.

X-rays and CT Scans

It is likely that every person who reads this book has had X-rays taken. They may have been dental X-rays, or X-rays for a broken bone or to try to locate an object that was accidentally swallowed. X-rays are high-energy **photons**, or particles of light. They are just like the photons that make up visible light, but they have more energy. This additional energy means that the photons are invisible to the eye, since the eye is only sensitive to photons from the red to violet range, while X-rays go beyond this range. More energy also means that the photons are able to penetrate material more easily.

For a patient with a broken arm, the doctor will expose the arm to X-rays, which pass through the arm to expose the film in a cassette that is placed underneath it. Because the bone is harder and denser than soft tissue like muscles, fewer of the X-rays will be able to pass through the bone enabling its image to be captured on X-ray film. In other words, the softer tissues are more transparent to X-rays than are the hard tissues.

When the X-rays hit the film, the hard tissues cast a shadow on the film. In areas where more photons hit, the film becomes more exposed and turns black, so the shadows left by the bones look white on the X-ray films. The area where the bone is broken will show up as a spot with a slightly higher (or maybe a slightly lower) density, represented by a darker or a lighter area on the film. Different internal organs have different compositions; for example, the muscle of the heart is denser and absorbs more X-rays than the lungs, and the bone of the ribs absorbs more X-rays than either of these. So, an X-ray image of the chest will show the ribs as having the lightest color, with the heart the next lightest, and the lungs the darkest. In a case where someone swallows an object like a quarter or a rock, the denser metal or rock will show up as being lighter in color than the stomach or intestines. A computed tomography (CT) scan is similar to an X-ray, except that a CT scanner provides an image of only a narrow slice—a few millimeters wide—of the body. By scanning a

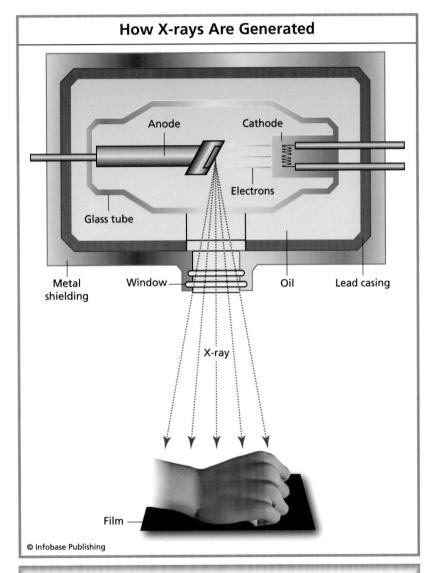

How X-rays Are Generated

© Infobase Publishing

Figure 7.1 X-rays are concentrated into a beam and reflected toward the object being photographed.

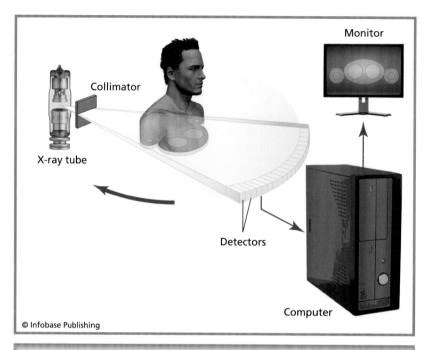

© Infobase Publishing

Figure 7.2 When a person gets a CT scan, an X-ray tube produces X-rays, while the collimator turns radiation into parallel beams. Detectors pick up thin slices of the total image, which, when combined, provide a detailed look at the body part being examined.

great many slices, the CT scanner can generate a very detailed image of a particular body part.

Because X-rays and CT scans expose the body to ionizing radiation, some have wondered if this radiation can, itself, be dangerous. Indeed, some scientists have wondered if X-rays might even cause cancer. Luckily, the amount of radiation dose from medical X-rays and CT scans is very low and is not harmful to the patient. It is also good to remember that doctors order X-rays to help them diagnose a problem: Not having that information can be dangerous. The risk of making an incorrect diagnosis is worse than the risk of cancer from having an X-ray or a CT scan. Before X-rays were available, doctors often had to cut open the body to find the source of the problem. X-rays have made such "exploratory surgery" all but obsolete, and this makes it safer for all patients.

Making X-rays

X-ray machines all work using the same principles. These principles are the same as those for a device known as a linear accelerator that is also used to treat cancer. In an X-ray machine, a beam of very fast electrons hurtles towards a metal target, which may be made of copper or tungsten. When the electrons hit the target, it is almost the same effect as making sparks by striking rocks against each other—except that, in this case, the "sparks" are X-rays. Faster-moving electrons hit the target harder and make higher-energy X-rays.

Nuclear Medicine and PET Scans

Sometimes X-rays and CT scans from outside the body cannot tell doctors what they need to know; sometimes they need to inject radioactive substances into the body to find out what is wrong. This is where nuclear medicine comes in. Suppose that a doctor has a patient who is eating everything in sight, but is still losing weight. Even after a thorough checkup, the doctor might need more information to figure out what is wrong. The patient's symptoms could be caused by a lot of things, so the doctor will want to make sure to provide the right treatment for the right condition. The doctor might order a nuclear medicine scan using radioactive iodine to see if the patient's thyroid gland is working properly. The thyroid gland absorbs iodine, so once the injected radioactive iodine has been absorbed, it lights up the thyroid with invisible high-energy photons called gamma rays that can be detected with a special camera. The nuclear medicine doctor then scans the patient's neck (where the thyroid is located) and takes a picture of the thyroid that will help to determine if the gland is working properly. The amount of iodine given for this sort of a scan—a diagnostic dose—will not give off enough radiation to damage the thyroid or to hurt the patient.

In this case, the nuclear medicine scan may reveal that the thyroid gland is too active, a condition that is called *hyperthyroidism*. The thyroid gland helps control how fast the body burns food, so an overly active thyroid can give someone too big of an appetite, even

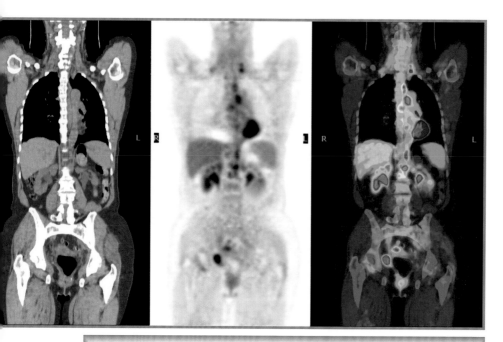

Figure 7.3 PET/CT fusion technology aids in the diagnosis of cancer. This PET/CT image shows many ganglionic metastases of ovarian cancer.

while the patient is losing weight. This can be a dangerous condition. One way to treat it is to give the patient an even larger dose of the radioactive iodine, a dose high enough to destroy the thyroid gland so it cannot cause any problems in the future. While the thyroid produces a hormone that is necessary for the body to work correctly, it is possible to substitute a medicine that will do the job. So, by using a high dose of radioactive iodine to destroy the thyroid, the other symptoms of hyperthyroidism, such as high appetite and weight loss, should both be cured.

Other body organs use different molecules in order to function. The brain, for example, uses a great deal of glucose (a form of sugar) for its energy, so adding radioactive atoms to sugar helps doctors to see how well parts of the brain are working. These radioactive atoms emit **positrons**—antimatter electrons—which will meet up with regular electrons. When positrons meet with electrons, they both vanish in a burst of gamma-ray energy; the gamma rays can be detected using a gamma camera similar to the one used for a thyroid scan. Parts of the brain that are active will use more glucose, and they will show up brighter on a **PET scan**. If a part of the brain is using more glucose than expected (which is common when cancer cells are present), it will show up on a PET scan. PET scans have also dramatically increased scientists' understanding of how the brain works by showing which parts of the brain use more glucose in performing everyday tasks, such as talking, listening, or thinking.

Radiation Oncology

As explained in Chapter 3, radiation can cause cancer, so it may be surprising to learn that radiation can also be used to treat cancer. Radiation can burn, so it is easy to understand that exposing a cancer to a high level of radiation can destroy it. This treatment is called radiation oncology (oncology is the science of cancer). The primary tools of a radiation oncologist are radioactive sources and linear accelerators. A radioactive source such as iodine-125, for example, can be inserted into a cancer, so the radiation it gives off will kill the cancer cells. Or the source can be located outside the body, but shielded in such a way that only a narrow beam of radiation is emitted. That beam of radiation can be aimed at the cancer to destroy it. This is called external beam therapy. A machine called a *linear accelerator* shoots a beam of high-energy electrons at a metal plate, which then responds by giving off an X-ray beam. This beam can be precisely controlled and shaped to conform exactly to the shape of the tumor. This helps to make sure that only the cancerous tissue is damaged without harming healthy tissue. Thanks to modern linear accelerators, many cancers can now be treated that were very difficult to treat with earlier technology.

RADIATION IN THE LABORATORY

Radioactivity can help in many forms of research. For example, scientists who are trying to develop a new drug to treat a liver disease will have to run a lot of tests before giving it to people. For example, they will need to know if the drug can be taken as a pill, or if it has to be injected into the body; a pill may be destroyed by

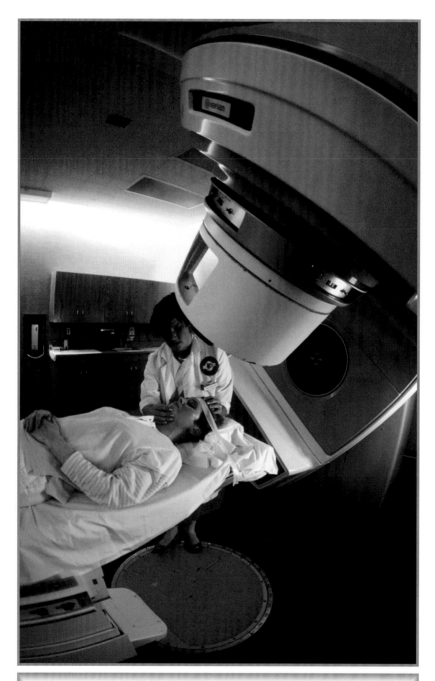

Figure 7.4 A technician uses a linear accelerator on a cancer patient for radiation treatment.

stomach acids before it has a chance to reach the liver and treat the disease. Scientists also need to know what happens to the drug in the body: How much of it goes to the liver? How much comes out in the urine and feces? Does the drug go to any other parts of the body? One way to answer these questions is by doing research using drugs that are labeled with radioactivity. By tracking the radioactivity, scientists can see how much of the drug actually goes to the liver, and whether it goes to any other part of the body where it might cause harm. Collecting a person's urine and feces can tell scientists how rapidly the drug leaves the body, which helps the scientists figure out how many pills patients should take and how often they need to take them.

Medical researchers often use radioactive tracers to trace the path of substances injected into the body. Radioactivity can also be used to trace the paths of nutrients inside of cells, or to see how pollutants (or fertilizers or other compounds) move through the environment. In fact, the use of radioactive tracers in research is similar to how nuclear medicine is used to diagnose disease, but for different reasons. The drugs and other compounds that researchers use are identical to "normal" ones with the exception that they have a single radioactive atom added to each molecule to make them easy to track through the body. Scientists and doctors have been successfully using radioactivity in this way in the laboratory for over half a century, and they are likely to continue doing so for many years to come.

RADIATION IN THE FACTORY

One of the properties of radiation is that it is absorbed by materials, just as X-rays are absorbed by the bones. Luckily, the amount of this **attenuation** can be predicted and calculated, so radiation measurements can be used to help control how a factory works. One simple way is called a tank-level gauge.

Suppose an operator is working with a tank that is designed to contain a dangerous chemical, like a form of acid, and needs to make sure that the tank does not overflow. In addition, there may be other problems if the tank empties out. The operator needs to be able to

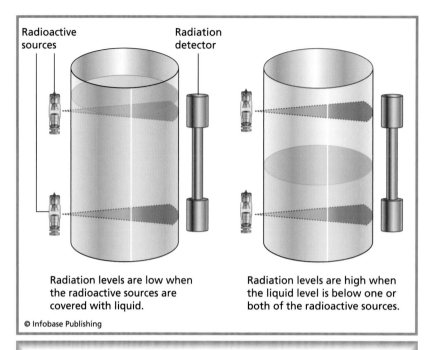

Radioactive sources

Radiation detector

Radiation levels are low when the radioactive sources are covered with liquid.

Radiation levels are high when the liquid level is below one or both of the radioactive sources.

© Infobase Publishing

Figure 7.5 Radiation detectors help indicate whether a tank filled with chemicals is about to overflow.

automatically see how full the tank is. Radioactivity provides a handy solution to this problem.

Remembering that material absorbs radiation, the operator puts two radioactive sources inside the tank of acid, one near the top and one near the bottom. Two radiation detectors are then placed outside the tank, one near each of the sources. If the acid is covering the radioactive source, the radiation levels will measure very low, and if the source is not covered with acid, radiation levels will be higher. So the upper source (the overflow warning) should always have high radiation levels, while the lower source (the tank empty warning) should always have low levels of radiation. If the tank level rises too high, covering the upper source, the radiation levels near the upper source will suddenly drop and the operators will know that they are in danger of having acid overflow, and so they can stop filling the tank. Or, if radiation levels measured by the lower gauge suddenly increase, it will warn the operators to either stop draining the tank, or to add more acid, to keep it from emptying out. The readings can also be measured by automated, computerized systems to control the tank level without human interference.

Radiation is also used in a similar manner to measure the thickness of steel, paper, tobacco, or other products. In the case of steel, it is known exactly how much radiation should penetrate a piece of steel to reach a detector. If radiation levels are too high, it means that the steel is too thin, so the operators will thicken the steel to the right measurement.

This chapter has only touched the surface of how radiation affects people's lives. It is true that radiation can cause harm, but it can be quite useful, and it can bring many benefits. In trying to decide if radiation and radioactivity are good or bad, one must

My Own Nuclear Medicine Scan by Andrew Karam

A few years ago, my doctor decided that I needed to have a nuclear medicine scan to see if my heart was working properly. I went to the hospital where the nurse injected me with two different forms of radioactivity—technetium-99 and thallium-201. While these went to, and through, my heart, the gamma camera took many pictures. Furthermore, the doctor, a friend of mine, was willing to spend time telling me what it all meant.

Some of the radioactivity was absorbed out of the blood by the heart itself. Luckily, the image showed that the entire heart was close to the same color—this meant that the whole heart was receiving blood, which meant that all of my coronary arteries (the blood vessels that supply blood to the heart tissue) were not plugged up and were working properly.

Because the blood was marked with radioactive tracers, the gamma camera was able to show how much of the blood inside the heart was pumped out again. This is called

(continues)

(continued)

the *ejection fraction*, and a high ejection fraction means that the heart is pumping blood effectively. In my case, the doctor and I were both happy to see that my heart was doing a good job of pumping blood around my body. The net result was that the doctor felt that my heart was in good shape, and we both stopped worrying.

After the scan, I made some measurements on myself with my own radiation instruments. I found out, for example, that my whole body was radioactive, but most of the radioactivity was coming from the areas of my liver and my bladder (in the urine). At first, the radiation levels from my body were as high as I normally measure in an X-ray room when an X-ray is being taken. Over the next two or three days, the short-lived technetium (which has a half-life of only six hours) vanished entirely, and, over the next few weeks, the longer-lived thallium also left my body. So, after a few weeks, the radiation levels from my body dropped to normal and I was no longer radioactive. And I was happy to know that I was also healthy and could expect to stay that way for many years.

consider not only the harm that they can do, but the good that comes from them as well. In fact, it is probably best to say that radiation is not good or bad in and of itself—it is a tool, and what makes this tool good or bad is how it is used.

8

Experiments with Radiation

Until now, this book has simply been explaining what radiation and radioactivity are, how they work, how they are used, and how they can affect us. Now it is time to have a little fun!

FINDING HELP WITH THE EXPERIMENTS

Finding an adult who knows a lot about radiation is much easier than one might think. Luckily, radiation or radioactivity is used in many everyday places that are likely to have someone who works full time with radiation. Here are some places to contact:

- Large universities, especially ones that do a lot of research; ask to speak with the "radiation safety officer"
- Many large hospitals, especially if they have programs in radiation oncology or nuclear medicine; again, ask to speak with the radiation safety officer
- If there is a nuclear power plant nearby, ask to speak with someone in "Health Physics" (the department that practices radiation safety)
- Go online to the Health Physics Society Web site (www.hps. org), then click on the link titled "Who we are/Organization/

Chapters," which will provide a list of HPS chapters; contact one of the people listed in a nearby chapter

- Most colleges and universities have physics departments and geology departments (also called earth science departments); many of the professors or graduate students in these departments are willing to work with middle school and high school students, and many of the professors also have radiation detectors
- Go to the Health Physics Society Web site and click on the "Ask the Experts" feature and post a question asking for help in finding someone to assist on these experiments.

Materials

The next step is to find some radioactive materials and some equipment that measure radioactivity. It is *very* important to make sure that the radioactive materials are safe.

Where to Find Radioactive Materials

Many things in everyday life are radioactive. However, the radioactivity of these objects is often too weak to detect with ordinary detectors. So, even though a smoke detector contains small amounts of radioactivity, a Geiger counter will not detect it. It is necessary to find something that is a little "hotter," or more radioactive, to use in the experiments. Here are some suggestions:

Many rocks and minerals are radioactive

Radioactive rocks and minerals can be found at most rock and mineral shows—many larger cities have at least one each year. It is possible to find radioactive specimens at museums as well. If a university is nearby, the geology department (or the earth sciences department) might have a collection of uranium minerals—in these cases, it might be possible to borrow some of their specimens to do the experiments; or a professor or graduate student may even be able to help with the experiments (be sure to get parental permission as well). Here is a list of some common minerals that contain enough uranium for easy experimenting and that are *not* dangerous. By the way, rocks labeled "uranium ore" do contain uranium, but usually not enough for the rocks to be useful in experiments.

Uraninite	Monazite
Betafite	Pitchblende
Torbernite	Thorite
Autunite	Thucolite
Carnotite	Samarskite

Some antiques are radioactive

Rock and mineral shows are not the only places in which to find radioactivity. Many antique shops also sell objects that contain some radioactivity. Again, these objects are not dangerous; the amount of radioactivity is easily detectable, but not enough to be harmful. Here are some things that might show up in an antique shop that might contain enough radioactivity for an experiment:

- Old glow-in-the-dark watches or clocks (radium in the paint)
- Orange Fiestaware (uranium in the paint)
- Some forms of enameled jewelry (many red, yellow, and orange glazes contain uranium)
- "Vaseline glass," a yellow-green glass that is made into beads, glasses, pitchers, trays, and more (uranium is used as the coloring agent)
- Some older, high-quality optical lenses (contain thorium).

Where to find a radiation detector

The best way to find a radiation detector is to borrow one from a local hospital, university, or nuclear power plant. Every radiation safety department has radiation detectors, and some may be willing to lend one out, or to provide assistance on these experiments. Here are the types of detectors to ask for:

- GM "pancake" probe—has a very good response to many kinds of radiation
- Sodium iodide probe—detects only gamma radiation, but is very sensitive

- Zinc sulfide probe—detects only alpha radiation, but is useful for some experiments
- MicroR meter—measures low levels of radiation with very great sensitivity.

It is fairly easy to find ionization chambers. They contain gases that detect radiation by turning into ions when the radiation strikes them (see Chapter 2). Unfortunately, these meters are set for a very high level of radiation and are not very useful for measuring normal radiation levels; therefore, they will be almost useless for these experiments, although they are still nice to play around with.

If a radiation detector is unavailable for borrowing, it is possible to purchase one. Online auction sites often list fairly good radiation detectors at a reasonable price.

After obtaining a radiation detector, it is necessary to make sure that it is working properly:

1. Hook up the cable from the meter to the probe.
2. Turn the switch to "Battery Test" or "Battery" and make sure that the needle moves to the right part of the scale—if it does not, try putting new batteries in the meter.
3. Turn on the sound (put the "Audio" switch in the "On" position).
4. Turn the selector switch from "On" to the highest scale (usually x1,000 or x10,000).
5. Hold the probe next to a radioactive source and make sure that the meter reading increases and the probe produces audible clicks; it might be necessary to move the switch to a lower setting to make the needle move.

EXPERIMENTS

Experiment 1:	Background radiation
Goal:	Measure the radiation levels in the surroundings
Materials:	Radiation detector (a Geiger counter and/or sodium iodide detector is best)
	Piece of paper for recording information
	Radioactive source (radioactive rock or one of the sources mentioned in the section titled "Where to Find Radioactive Materials")

Procedure:

1. First, check the radiation detector to make sure it is operating properly.
   a. With the meter turned off, attach the cable to both the detector and the meter.
   b. Turn the switch to "Battery Test" (or push the "Battery Test" button).
   c. See that the needle moves to the "Battery Test" position.
   d. If it does not, check to make sure that the batteries are inserted properly; if so, insert new batteries.
   e. If there is an audio switch, turn it to "On."
2. Turn the meter switch to the highest scale setting (it should read "x1,000" or "x100") and wait about 20 to 30 seconds. The meter should click or beep; what does the meter read?
3. Turn the meter switch to the next lower scale setting. Is there a reading yet?
4. Continue turning the meter switch down until the needle is between the lowest number (usually the number 1) and the highest number (usually 5 or 6).
5. What is the count rate? Write this number on the paper. With a Geiger counter, it should be between 50 to 100 counts per minute (cpm); with a sodium iodide detector, it may be as low as 500 cpm, or as high as 10,000 cpm, depending on the size of the detector.

6. If other detectors are being used, repeat these steps and write down the reading.

7. Now go outside and repeat all of this again. Are the readings any different?

8. In a brick home, make radiation measurements close to a brick wall (less than 1 foot [30 cm] away) and again at least 25 feet (7.6 m) away. Is there a difference in the readings? (Some bricks and some concrete contain clays that are somewhat radioactive, meaning there are much higher readings closer to brick or concrete.)

9. Finally, perform these same readings in the basement (if one is available). Are the readings higher or lower? Actually, there is no way to predict this; while the concrete walls might increase background radiation levels, being underground might block cosmic radiation, so the readings may increase, decrease, or even remain the same.

This experiment demonstrates the presence of measurable radiation in nature. As the experiments show, different detectors will give different readings, even if the radiation field remains the same. Finally, materials in buildings sometimes have an effect on background radiation levels—in fact, this is not uncommon.

Experiment 2:	The effects of distance on radiation
Goal:	Learn how radiation levels can drop (or increase) drastically when the detector moves away from (or toward) the source
Materials:	Geiger counter
	Radioactive source
	Ruler, tape measure, or meter stick
	Paper and pencil
	Graph paper

Procedure:

1. Put the radioactive source (rock, Fiestaware, etc.) on a desk or table, next to a ruler, tape measure, or meter stick at a distance of 6 inches (15 cm).

2. Turn on the radiation detector to the appropriate scale (one that has a reading between the highest and lowest numbers).

3. Put the probe next to the "0" mark (the beginning of the ruler) and write down the meter reading.

4. Move the radioactive source in to a distance of 3 inches (7.5 cm) and write down the meter reading.

5. Move the source out to distances of 9, 12, 15, and 24 inches (22, 30, 37, and 60 cm) and write down the readings at each distance. Keep moving the source to greater distances as long as it still produces at least a few hundred counts on the meter.

6. Now, set up the graph paper to show distance on the bottom (the x-axis) and the number of counts on the side (the y-axis).

7. For each distance, plot the number of counts.

8. Now connect these points. Is it a curve? A line? What is the shape?

9. What does this mean? How quickly does the radiation dose change by moving closer or farther away?

This experiment demonstrates that radiation falls off quickly the further away the object is from the detector. In fact, at double the distance, the count rate should be lower by a factor of 4; at three times the distance, it should be lower by a factor of 9. This means that when people are exposed to radiation, moving away will cause their radiation **dose rate** to drop pretty quickly.

Experiment 3:	The effects of different kinds of shielding
Goal:	Determine the best material for blocking the radiation source
Materials:	Geiger counter
	Radioactive source
	Piece of paper
	Piece of aluminum foil
	Brick
	A thick book

Procedure:

1. Place the radioactive source (rock or Fiestaware) on the table and the detector (Geiger tube) about a foot away. (If the count rate is less than about 500 counts per minute, try moving the detector closer.)
2. Write down the number of counts on the meter.
3. Now put a piece of paper in front of the rock and write down the number of counts. Do the same with the piece of aluminum foil. Try folding the foil several times and see if the counts go down a little more.
4. Now put a hand in front of the radiation source and write down the number of counts.
5. Finally, put the book, and then the brick in front of the source and write down the number of counts again.
6. What are the results? What made the biggest difference in the number of counts? Was there any object that did not change the count rate much? What made the biggest difference in the count rate?

This experiment demonstrates that different things absorb radiation differently. Putting a brick in the path of the radiation should have produced the biggest drop in the number of counts, which would indicate that the brick is the strongest shield. A thick book should provide the next highest amount of shielding, followed by a hand. If the detector is sensitive enough, the aluminum foil should provide a little more shielding than the paper, but the equipment might not be able to detect the difference.

Experiment 4:	Count rate versus dose rate—advanced (requires more detectors)
Goal:	Find out how different detectors respond differently to radiation
Materials:	Geiger counter
	Sodium iodide detector
	Ion chamber
	Radioactive source

Procedure:

1. Put the radioactive source on the table.
2. Hook up the Geiger counter in another room and write down the number of counts: This is the amount of "background" radiation that the detector measures.
3. Now turn off the meter and attach the sodium iodide detector; again, write down the number of background counts.
4. Finally, turn on the ion chamber and, with the switch on the lowest setting, write down the dose rate (it should be close to zero).
5. Now bring in the radioactive source and put it on the table, close to the detectors.
6. Hold the Geiger counter about one-half inch (12 millimeters) above the source and write down the number of counts.
7. Hold the sodium iodide detector about one-half inch (12 mm) above the source and write down the number of counts.
8. Now hold the ion chamber about one-half inch (12 mm) above the source and write down the dose rate.
9. What is the difference between the sodium iodide detector and the Geiger tube? Why is there this difference? After all, everything is identical except for the detector. Are some detectors simply more sensitive than others?
10. Why is there not much of a response (maybe none at all) with the ion chamber?

This experiment demonstrates that different kinds of radiation detectors respond differently to the exact same source of radiation—some kinds of detectors are sensitive to different kinds of radiation, and some detectors are simply more sensitive to radiation than others are. So, just because there is a high number of counts (or a lot of clicks) does not mean anything, unless one knows what kind of detector is being used. This experiment also shows that it is possible to measure background radiation, and that different detectors measure it differently. Finally, a lot of radiation counts do not give a high radiation dose rate. This is important to know because of the potential dangers that may arise from the radiation dose rate. It does not matter how many counts there are; as long as the dose rate is low, the risk is low. The body can easily repair the damage from radiation, as long as the radiation streams in slowly enough, as is the case with the radiation in any of the objects used in the experiments discussed in this chapter.

9

What Have We Learned?

Radiation exists everywhere. Background radiation comes from outer space and is found everywhere on Earth. No one can get away from it, no matter how hard they try. Still, these low levels of background radiation appear to have had no ill effects on living things for the entire history of life on Earth.

There are many specific sources of radiation—in nature, it is found in the elements uranium, thorium, and potassium in the rocks and soils. When uranium and thorium decay, they produce radon, radium, and other radioactive products. Radiation also comes from the potassium within in the human body. All of these natural sources of radiation give someone who lives in North America a dose of about 0.01 mSv (1 mrem) each day—about one-tenth of a chest X-ray. But the doses can vary a lot from place to place on the planet, even reaching about 5 to 100 times that amount in parts of Brazil, China, India, and Iran.

People are also exposed to radiation from man-made sources, such as medicine, some consumer products, and nuclear power plants. Radiation is a tool in saving many lives. Intense beams of radiation are used in cancer therapy to destroy tumors in all parts of the body. Growing numbers of cancer patients are being completely cured.

But there have been some accidents involving radioactivity, such as the Chernobyl nuclear power plant accident. These incidents have released radioactivity into the environment, where it has spread into the food chain. Even so, the populations of plants and animals living near Chernobyl have reached new highs in spite of high radiation doses.

Radiation can cause harm, but it takes a fairly high dose to cause any damage to the body that cannot be repaired. Of course, at higher levels of exposure, it can be dangerous, but the good news is that it is very unusual for anyone to be exposed to dangerously high radiation levels. In other words, radiation is like many other tools—it can be harmful if it is misused, but if it is treated carefully, it can be used safely.

Nuclear power plants produce radiation. Nuclear energy produces about 20% of the electricity in the United States and about 16% worldwide. Unlike most ways of producing electricity, these plants do not release the carbon dioxide that causes global warming and climate change. The great majority of the time, nuclear power plants operate as they were designed and do no harm to anyone. Even so, some accidents have taken place at nuclear power plants. The Chernobyl accident killed 31 people at the time, and the large doses of radiation that it released may cause more deaths in the future. Fortunately, there are no nuclear power plants in the United States that are built like Chernobyl, so U.S. nuclear reactors cannot have the same kind of accident. The worst accident in the United States took place at the Three Mile Island plant. Although this destroyed the nuclear reactor, nobody at the plant or in the surrounding community was hurt by the radiation that was released because of how the plant was designed.

Nuclear weapons are the most dangerous source of radiation, and they have been used twice in combat. Each time, many tens of thousands of people were killed, and many more were injured. There were many "open air" tests of nuclear weapons in the 1940s, 1950s, and early 1960s, but the 1963 Nuclear Test-Ban Treaty put a stop to that; since it went into effect, all nuclear weapons tests have been conducted underground.

Radioactivity entering the environment can find many pathways to humans. Radioactivity emitted into the air, for example, may be breathed in. But it can also settle into people's drinking water; or, it can settle onto plants to be eaten by cows and ingested by persons who eat the plants, drink the cows' milk, or eat their beef. There are a great many different ways that radioactivity can escape from, say, a radioactive waste site or a nuclear power plant. However, an entire chain of events must take place for this to happen, and the more links in that chain, the weaker the radiation dose becomes before it finally reaches people.

Radiation and radioactivity have many positive uses. As mentioned before, radiation is used in medicine to help to diagnose or to treat diseases. It is also used in industry to help control tank levels or the thickness of steel, among other things. Some radioactivity ends up in consumer products—in some cases (such as smoke detectors) because the radioactivity makes them work better. In other cases, products are made of substances that happen to contain small amounts of radioactivity (such as the natural radioactivity found in clays or minerals).

For many reasons, it is important to handle radiation and radioactivity with great care because high levels of exposure to them can cause great harm. But radiation is no more dangerous than many other things people use, or do, on an everyday basis (such as cars or playing certain sports). So, the best way to think about radiation is that it should be treated carefully. People do not need to be scared of it. As long as it is used carefully, it is not dangerous. In fact, it can do good things without creating danger. Like many other things in life, it is a useful tool, as long as it is handled with proper care.

Glossary

Alpha particle   A type of radiation consisting of four particles (two neutrons and two protons joined together), released from some kinds of radioactive material. Alpha radiation does not penetrate material well, and can be stopped by a sheet of paper or the outer dead layer of skin.

Atom   A building block of matter consisting of a core (the nucleus) surrounded by particles known as electrons.

Attenuation   The reduction of exposure rate upon passage of radiation through matter.

Background radiation   Ionizing radiation that occurs naturally in the environment, including cosmic radiation; radiation emitted in air, water, soil, and rock.

Beta radiation   A kind of radiation consisting of a particle known as an electron, released by certain radioactive materials. Beta radiation does not penetrate matter highly. The highest-energy beta radiation can be stopped by a few centimeters of plastic or aluminum.

Chain reaction   A multi-stage nuclear reaction in which the fission of one nucleus releases particles that trigger fissions in other nearby nuclei.

Cleanup   Decontamination and removal of radioactive or other hazardous materials from a contaminated site.

Contamination   The unwanted deposit of radioactive material in an environment.

Control rods   The rods in a nuclear reactor that help slow down and control nuclear reactions and the release of energy.

Cosmic radiation   Particles of matter and light (such as X-rays and gamma rays) coming from space or produced when these objects interact with the Earth's atmosphere.

Critical mass   The smallest amount of radioactive material needed to start a nuclear chain reaction that continues by itself once it is started.

Daughter nuclide   A lighter radioactive particle formed from the nuclear transformation of a heavier radioactive particle referred to as its "parent."

Decay product   A lighter nucleus that results from the decay of a heavier nucleus.

Dirty bomb   See radiological dispersal device.

Disposal   Placement of waste in a facility designed to keep waste from entering the environment.

DNA   The molecule that contains genetic material in living things; short for deoxyribonucleic acid.

Dose   The amount of exposure to nuclear radiation.

Dose rate   The amount of dose over a given time; often expressed as an average over some time period (e.g., a year or a lifetime).

Electron   A negatively charged subatomic particle; electrons surround the nucleus of an atom.

Element   A particular kind of atom as defined by its number of protons; for example, the hydrogen atom is an element that contains one proton.

Exposure   A general term describing contact with ionizing radiation.

Exposure pathway   The means of intake of a substance by an organism (for example, inhalation or ingestion).

Gamma radiation (gamma rays)   An invisible, high-energy form of light (electromagnetic radiation). Gamma rays penetrate matter easily and require thick shielding as a guard—for example, up to 1 meter of concrete or a few tens of centimeters of steel.

Geiger counter A device that measures radiation by counting the number of "clicks" produced by electrons in a radioactive sample.

Gray A unit of measurement that describes how much ionizing radiation is absorbed by the body. 1 Gy = 100 rad.

Groundwater Water below the land surface.

Half-life Time required for a material to reduce the radioactivity it releases to 50%, or half, of its original rate. Half-lives of radioactive materials vary from millionths of a second to billions of years.

High-level radioactive waste Highly radioactive material that requires permanent isolation. Examples of high-level waste include any used nuclear reactor fuel, and any of the waste that is produced when reactor fuel is recycled.

Homogeneous Something that is uniform in composition, such as mashed potatoes, as opposed to something that is inhomogeneous, such as raisin bread.

Internal radioactivity Exposure received from a source of ionizing radiation inside of the body.

Ion An electrically charged atom or molecule.

Ionization The process by which a neutral atom loses an electron, turning the atom into a charged ion.

Ionizing radiation Any radiation capable of removing electrons from atoms or molecules, thereby turning them into ions.

Isotopes Different forms of a chemical element distinguished by having different numbers of neutrons in the atomic nucleus. A single atomic element generally has numerous isotopes. Some isotopes of an element may be stable, and others may be unstable (radioactive).

Low-level radioactive waste Material that produces radioactivity at low rates when compared with high-level radioactive waste.

Molecule An object consisting of two or more atoms joined together.

Neutron Uncharged particle normally found in the core (nucleus) of an atom or molecule; when released from the nucleus, it can strike another nucleus and cause it to fission (split).

Nuclear Having to do with the nucleus, or core, of an atom or molecule.

Nuclear fission   The act of splitting a nucleus into smaller pieces or fragments; this process releases a lot of energy.

Nuclear medicine   The use of radionuclides to diagnose and treat disease.

Nuclear reactor   A device that releases energy in a controlled fashion by splitting nuclei into smaller pieces.

Nuclear weapon   A device that releases an enormous amount of energy by either splitting nuclei into smaller parts or joining nuclei together.

Nucleus (plural, **nuclei**)   The positively charged core of an atom or molecule.

Nuclide   Any type of atom with a particular number of protons or neutrons.

Organic   In chemistry and physics, something that contains carbon atoms, which are the building blocks of life.

Parent nuclide   A larger radioactive nucleus that disintegrates into or releases a smaller (daughter) radioactive nucleus.

PET scan   A diagnostic medical image taken with a device that records gamma radiation from the body emitted when electrons combine with positrons that come from chemicals injected into the bloodstream.

Photon   A particle of light or other electromagnetic radiation; some photons are visible, such as yellow photons, while others are invisible, such as gamma ray or X-ray photons.

Positron   The antimatter counterpart to an electron: much lighter than a proton but with the same positive charge as a proton.

Proton   A positively charged particle in the nucleus of an atom.

Rad   A unit of measurement that describes how much ionizing radiation is absorbed by the body; 1 rad = 0.01 Gray.

Radiation   Energy released in the form of particles or waves; see also ionizing radiation.

Radioactive   An object that releases high-energy particles such as X-rays.

Radioactive decay   The transformation of an unstable nucleus into another kind of nucleus.

Radioactive waste   Solid, liquid, or gaseous radioactive material that is created as a byproduct of nuclear or industrial process; must be regulated as a hazardous material.

Radiological dispersal device (RDD)   A device designed to spread radioactive material through a detonation of conventional explosives or by other means.

Radiolytic   Refers to any process that uses radiation to split molecules into their constituent atoms or ions.

Radionuclide   A particular nucleus, as defined by the number of protons and neutrons that it contains.

Radon   A colorless, odorless, naturally occurring, and radioactive gaseous element formed by radioactive decay of isotopes of radium.

Reactor core   The center of a reactor where nuclear reactions take place, releasing energy.

Rem   A unit of measurement that describes the biological damage done by radiation when it is absorbed by the body; 1 rem = 0.01 Sievert.

Remediation   Action taken to reduce risks to human health or the environment posed by the presence of radioactive or hazardous chemical contaminants at a site including, but not restricted to, excavation of contaminated soil, removal of contaminants from building surfaces or equipment, stabilization of buried waste, and installation of engineered barriers (e.g., caps on waste trenches) to reduce the potential for migration of contaminants (see also cleanup).

Sievert   A unit of measurement that describes the biological damage done by radiation when it is absorbed in the body; 1 Sv = 100 rem.

Stable   A nonradioactive element; an element that does not decay into another element.

Strong nuclear force   The force that holds together a nucleus.

X-ray   A form of electromagnetic radiation that has high energy and is invisible; often used to take pictures inside the body.

Bibliography

Brinton, Turner. "U.S. Residents' Exposure to Medical Radiation 6 Times Higher than in 1980," American Institute of Physics Web site. Available online. URL: http://insidescience.org/reports/2007/010.html.

Draganic, Ivan G., Zorica G. Draganic, and Jean-Pierre Adloff. *Radiation and Radioactivity on Earth and Beyond*. Boca Raton, Fla.: CRC Press, 1993.

Fentiman, Audeen W., Brian K. Hajek, and Joyce E. Meredith. "What Are the Sources of Ionizing Radiation?" The Ohio State University Web site. Available online. URL: http://www.ag.ohio-state.edu/~rer/rerhtml/rer_22.html.

Fermi, Enrico. "Enrico Fermi's Own Story." *Chicago Sun-Times*, November 23, 1952. Available online URL: http://www.osti.gov/accomplishments/pdf/DE00782931/30.pdf.

Hester, J. Jeff, Steven J. Desch, Kevin R. Healy, et al. "The Cradle of the Solar System." *Science* 304 (May 21, 2004): 1116–1117.

International Atomic Energy Agency. *Energy, Electricity and Nuclear Power Estimates for the Period up to 2030*. Vienna, Austria: International Atomic Energy Agency, 2006.

International Atomic Energy Agency. *Nuclear Technology Review 2007*. Vienna, Austria: International Atomic Energy Agency, 2007.

Meshik, A.P., C. M. Hohenberg, and O. V. Pravdivtseva. "Record of Cycling Operation of the Natural Nuclear Reactor in the Oklo/Okelobondo Area in Gabon." *Physical Review Letters* 93 (October 29, 2004): 182302.

National Academies of Engineering and U.S. Department of Homeland Security. "Nuclear Attack," National Academies of Engineering Web site. Available online. URL: http://www.nae.edu/NAE/pubundcom.nsf/weblinks/CGOZ-6DZLNU/$file/nuclear%20attack%2006.pdf.

National Academies of Engineering and U.S. Department of Homeland Security. "Radiological Attack: Dirty Bombs and Other Devices," National Academies of Engineering Web site. Available online. URL:

http://www.nae.edu/NAE/pubundcom.nsf/weblinks/CGOZ-646NVG/
$file/radiological%20attack%2006.pdf.

National Council on Radiation Protection. *Report #93, Ionizing Radiation
Exposure of the Population of the United States.* Bethesda, Md.: NCRP
Publishers, 1987.

National Council on Radiation Protection. *Report #100, Exposure of the
U.S. Population from Diagnostic Medical Radiation.* Bethesda, Md.:
NCRP Publishers, 1988.

National Council on Radiation Protection. "Medical Radiation Exposure
of the U.S. Population: Preliminary Results from NCRP Scientific Committee 6-2 & Other Related Issues." Available online. URL: http://www.
ncrponline.org/PPFs/ICR_2008_DAS.pdf.

National Council on Radiation Protection. *Report #101, Exposure of the
U.S. Population from Occupational Radiation.* Bethesda, Md.: NCRP
Publishers, 1989.

Radiation Information Network, Idaho State University. "Food Irradiation," Idaho State University Web site. Available online. URL: http://
www.physics.isu.edu/radinf/food.htm.

Ravilious, Kate. "Despite Mutations, Chernobyl Wildlife Is Thriving." National Geographic News Web site. Available online. URL: http://news.
nationalgeographic.com/news/2006104/0426_060426_chernobyl.html.

Rhodes, Richard. *The Making of the Atomic Bomb.* New York: Simon and
Schuster, 1986.

Rogovin, M., and George T. Frampton. *Three Mile Island. a Report to the
Commissioners and to the Public.* Washington D.C.: Nuclear Regulatory
Commission, 1980.

Saling, James. *Radioactive Waste Management.* Boca Raton, Fla.: CRC
Press, 2001.

Sanger, David E. "North Korea Says It Tested a Nuclear Device Underground." *New York Times* (October 9, 2006): p. A1.

Savage, David, ed. *The Scientific and Regulatory Basis for the Geological
Disposal of Radioactive Waste.* New York: John Wiley and Sons, 1996.

Seaborg, G.T., and Walter D. Loveland. *The Elements Beyond Uranium.*
New York: John Wiley and Sons, Inc., 1990.

Segre, Emilio. *Enrico Fermi, Physicist.* Chicago: University of Chicago Press,
1970.

Shapiro, Jacob. *Radiation Protection,* 2nd. ed. Cambridge, Mass.: Harvard
University Press, 1981.

Shleien, Bernard, ed. *The Health Physics and Radiological Health Handbook.* Silver Spring, Md.: Scinta, Inc., 1992.

Teodorsson, Sven-Tage. *Anaxagoras' Theory of Matter*. Goteborg, Sweden: Acta Universitatis Gothoburgensis, 1992.

United Nations Scientific Committee on the Effects of Atomic Radiation. *Sources and Effects of Ionizing Radiation*. New York: United Nations, 2000.

U.S. Department of Energy. *The First Reactor*. Washington, D.C.: U.S. Government Printing Office, 1982.

U.S. Department of Health, Education and Welfare. *Radiological Health Handbook*. Washington, D.C.: U.S. Government Printing Office, 1970.

World Health Organization. "Health Effects of the Chernobyl Accident," World Health Organization Web site. Available online. URL: http://www.who.int/ionizing_radiation/chernobyl/en/.

Further Resources

Curie, Eve. *Madame Curie: A Biography.* Vincent Sheean, trans. Cambridge, Mass.: Da Capo Press, 2001.

Fox, Karen. *The Chain Reaction: Pioneers of Nuclear Science.* London: Franklin Watts, 1998.

Karam, P. Andrew, and Ben P. Stein. *Radical Radiation! Life in the Atomic Age.* Orlando, Fla.: Harcourt Achieve, 2007.

Kidd, J.S. et al. *Nuclear Power: The Study of Quarks and Sparks.* New York: Chelsea House, 2006.

Stwertka, Albert. *A Guide to the Elements.* New York: Oxford University Press USA, 2002.

Web Sites

Lawrence Berkeley National Laboratory. The Particle Adventure.
http://particleadventure.org/
> *Learn about the different particles and forces in nature.*

Lawrence Berkeley National Laboratory. The ABCs of Nuclear Science.
http://www.lbl.gov/abc/
> *Features a visual wall chart that shows the basics of nuclear science.*

Thinkquest. Atomic Alchemy: Nuclear Processes.
http://library.thinkquest.org/17940/
> *Discover more about nuclear reactions and the inventions and history of atomic science.*

U.S. Department of Energy. Internal Exposure from Radioactivity in Food and Beverages, U.S. Department of Energy Web site.
http://www.ocrwm.doe.gov/curriculum/unit2/pdf/lesson3activity3.pdf
> *Find out about the small amounts of naturally occurring radiation in food and beverages.*

Washington State Department of Health. "Typical Patient Exposures." Washington State Department of Health, Office of Radiation Protection.
http://www.doh.wa.gov/ehp/rp/xray/patientexp.htm
> Learn about different medical procedures that use radiation, and how much radiation exposure results from each procedure.

Picture Credits

Index

About the Authors

P. Andrew Karam is a scientist, writer, and educator who has devoted himself to radiation safety since 1981. He received his Ph.D. in environmental sciences from the Ohio State University. He has written over 100 technical articles and editorials in scientific and technical journals and newsletters. He has also authored over 200 encyclopedia articles and several books, including *Rig Ship for Ultra Quiet*, which describes his first encounters with radiation science as a Navy technician on a nuclear submarine. He lives in Rochester, New York, with his wife, five children, and an assortment of pets.

Ben P. Stein has been a professional science writer since 1992. He earned his bachelor's degree with honors at the State University of New York at Binghamton. He then attended journalism school at New York University, where he embarked upon a career in science writing. He worked at the American Institute of Physics for 16 years. His writing has appeared in *Encyclopedia Britannica*, *Popular Science*, *New Scientist*, *Salon*, and many other publications. He lives with his wife, son, and two stepsons.